Contents

Foreword

My favorite thing about sewing is that I can always make something just the way I want it.

For instance, have you ever had a bag you didn't like? I have. Too many to count. Usually, the problem is that the straps are too long or too short, or too wide or too skinny. Sometimes it has to with the pockets. Either there aren't enough, there are too many, or they're all in the wrong places. If it's not one thing it's another. I have spent countless hours scouring stores for the perfect bag only to go home empty handed and return to a trusty old handmade bag, even if it's virtually falling apart at the seams from years of love and use.

That's why I like to make my own bags, especially from one of Michelle's patterns. Her instructions are crystal clear, and her designs are perfection. She has thought of it all when it comes to creating a fashionable, yet functional, bag. She's a bag genius! It's thanks to her years of designing and sewing magnificent wedding gowns for particular brides. They not only gave her experience when it comes to fine details, but expertise as well.

Every bag you sew made from a Golightly Studio's pattern will be an instant favorite and an instant hit! Be careful how much you flaunt it, because you'll be asked to sew one for just about everyone you know. But then again, maybe that's a good thing.

Happy sewing!

Chelsea Andersen of Pink Fig Design

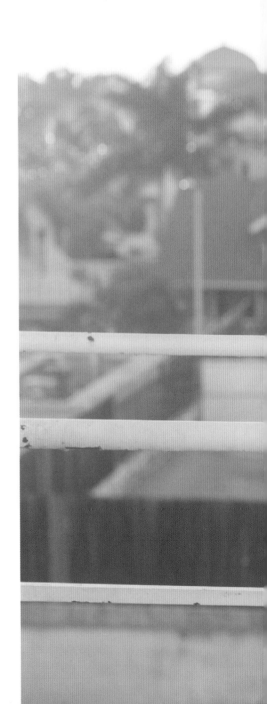

Signature Bags

12 Trend-Setting Bag Patterns to Sew at Home

MICHELLE GOLIGHTLY
MARY GAVILANES (ILLUSTRATOR)

Fons&Porter
CINCINNATI, OHIO

Introduction

For most of us, melting into the middle of ordinary is not one of our goals. Just the opposite, we want to express our emotions, attitudes, opinions and passions. Few things create a more visual statement of who a woman is than what she wears and how she accessorizes. Using her appearance as an expression of self creates a signature look. It can be a one-of-a-kind, never-been-seen style reflecting her uniqueness, individual moods, pallette and essence. As sewers we have an advantage in achieving this signature look.

My collection of patterns takes current fashion styles and transforms them into something an average sewer can make. Sign your name to your project by thoughtfully considering the fabrics, textures and embellishments. These patterns provide an avenue with which to experiment with a variety of materials and hardware.

To stand out from other handmade bags, and to create a level of professionalism and edginess, I incorporated a variety of hardware (see Resources for available kits). As you consider which projects to make and the availability of hardware, notice that several patterns have either no hardware or options for limiting hardware.

In addition to creating a personal signature, these patterns meet your needs for function without sacrificing style. They have pockets and zippers where they can be useful, and they include straps, handles and closures that will make these bags your favorite accessories. The designs range from clutches to travel bags.

How many people look at a fashionable bag and think, "That's beautiful, but I could never sew it?" In contrast, an 11-year-old girl named Jenna called me a while ago wanting to know if I would teach her to sew a quilt. Her attitude was not, "I could never make a quilt," but, "Can you teach me?" I want to capture that young, motivated attitude, creating an "I can do that" confidence with sewers of all levels. No matter your skill level, there are patterns in this collection with which you will succeed. And with each success comes courage and knowledge to dive into another project.

Each pattern begins with a level of difficulty indicator, but don't let that deter you from making the bag you want. Use patience, a slow pace and confidence. Throw in every bit of your imagination, and my patterns will take you successfully to the finish.

To be honest, sometimes we create just for the fun of creating. Like a musician composing a never-before heard melody, or an artist signing an original canvas, create your own artistic signature. Join our sewing adventure.

Getting Started

To help you succeed with these patterns, this section of general instructions is included. A careful review of the information will be helpful. After reading, you will understand my style of thinking, the terminology and the materials used.

About This Book

This section addresses subjects of general interest that apply to all of the patterns. *Please read thoroughly.*

In each pattern:

- When a piece is first used, it will be in CAPS.
- For simplification and clarity, stabilizers (Soft and Stable, fusible fleece, and woven fusible interfacing) are not shown in most illustrations.
- The illustrations show stacked layers slightly offset so you can identify the number of layers involved in that particular step. If there is a question, refer to the written text.
- Unless otherwise indicated, the seam allowance is ½" (1.3cm).
- Read through all pattern instructions before beginning.
- Tips are included in the text of each pattern.
- The CD includes pattern pieces for you to print, a Cutting Chart for each pattern (especially helpful for the patterns with many pieces) and instructions on how to print and assemble your pattern pieces.

Pattern Difficulty

Pattern difficulty is identified at the beginning of each pattern. Four levels range from beginning (first projects, few skills and few steps) to experienced (able to follow patterns with complicated sewing and finishing techniques). Because some of these patterns are for beginners, the instructions and tips might seem elementary at times. I tried to be thoughtful regarding the difficulty rating of each pattern, but in the end, it's a subjective judgment. One thing I can guarantee—if you are patient and careful, you can sew all of these patterns.

Materials

The first step toward a positive outcome is to choose the correct tools, hardware and materials. The information in this section can help you make informed decisions and set the stage for achievement.

Fabric Tips

Substituting fabric: Each pattern includes fabric choice suggestions. Think through every step to the end if considering a fabric that's not in the list of suggestions. If sewing quilting cotton on a bag designed for home décor or laminated cotton, fuse one layer of woven fusible interfacing to the wrong side of each piece before beginning. Omit woven fusible interfacing if sewing home décor or laminated cotton with a pattern designed for quilting cotton.

Directional fabric: Sometimes it's fun to use directional fabric. To ensure the fabric will be consistent with the design, visualize the finished use for each piece before cutting. Additional yardage might be required.

Fabric protection: All of these bags use cotton fabric. Some kind of weather/fabric protection should be applied. Follow product directions. For bags like the *Clear-as-Day Tote* (page 116), treat the pieces prior to sewing so the product doesn't get on the clear vinyl.

Prewash: If you plan to wash the bag or even "spot" wash it, prewash your fabric. Check the fiber content to get proper washing instructions.

Tools

These tools will be helpful for completing some projects, but they are not needed for every pattern:

- ⅜" (1cm) eyelet/grommet tool
- ¼" (6mm) eyelet/grommet tool
- Screwdriver
- Hammer
- Needle-nose pliers
- Craft knife
- Seam ripper
- Safety pins
- Pinking shears
- Piping or zipper foot
- Embroidery scissors
- Rotary cutter and mat
- Narrow machine needles and silk pins for laminate cotton sewing
- Denim topstitch machine needles for denim repurposing

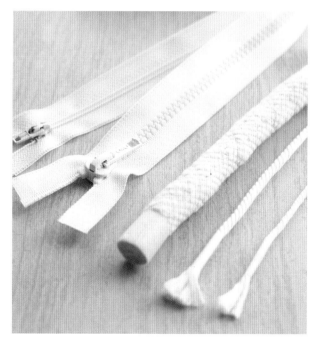

Zippers and Cording

laminated cotton, quilting cotton, home décor weight cotton

Fabric, Notions and Stabilizers

Most of these materials can be purchased at craft or fabric shops:

Bias binding (bias tape): There are two widths of bias tape in this book: extra-wide double-fold ½" (1.3cm) bias tape, and double-fold ¼" (6mm) bias tape.

Cable cord and piping cord: Made of cotton or polyester. Three thicknesses are used in these patterns: ³⁄₃₂" (2.4mm), ⁵⁄₃₂" (4mm) and ²²⁄₃₂" (1.7cm).

Clear vinyl (CV): Clear vinyl thickness is indicated by gauge. The 10-gauge is lighter and more flexible than the 20-gauge.

Elastic: Two widths of braided elastic are used in the book: ¾" (2cm) and ¼" (6mm).

Fusible fleece (FF): Try Pellon, Quilting Interfacing-Fleece, TP971F Fusible Thermolam Plus.

Glue: For extra security on twist lock hardware, use E-6000 industrial strength adhesive. For gluing into a purse frame, use Beacon 527 Multi-use Glue.

Home décor fabrics: Home décor fabrics are heavier than quilting cotton, but they come in a variety of weights. Often they have a more noticeable weave.

Laminate (laminated cotton): This fabric comes with a laminated coating already covering the cotton.

Peltex: One-sided fusible Peltex is good for strength, especially in the bottom of the bag. Pellon, Crafts & Home Décor Interfacing-Stabilizer, 71F Peltex Ultra Firm 1-Sided fusible is great. There are other products available for strength, but Peltex has been chosen here because it is easily available.

Interfacing: Soft and Stable, woven fusible interfacing, fusible fleece, Peltex

Quilting cotton (QT): Any cotton can be used, but the higher quality quilting cotton is sturdier and more durable.

Soft and Stable (SS): Soft and Stable from By Annie has the unique quality of holding its shape while remaining soft. If it gets creased, use a steam iron on it. You can use fusible fleece instead, but the strength of the shape will not be as pronounced.

When pinning into SS, you often do not need to send the pins all the way through the thickness. If you catch only the fabric and top layer of SS with the pins, there will be less buckling, leaving a smoother look after sewing. Do not piece Soft and Stable.

A similar product, although a little less sturdy, is FF77 Flex-Form Sew-In by Pellon.

Woven fusible interfacing (WFI): Woven interfacing is preferable because it doesn't buckle like some other fusible stabilizers. Try Pellon, Apparel Interfacing Specialty, SF 101 Shape-Flex Fusible.

Zippers: All-purpose zippers are indicated as "zipper." Zippers with larger teeth are indicated as "sport zipper." Avoid using zippers with metal teeth except for in the *On-the-Go Bag* (page 136), because they are too difficult to topstitch. Almost any zipper can be shortened. Sew the zipper in place first. Cut off the zipper end, leaving about ½" (1.3cm) extra. Whipstitch near the end several times for security.

Purse Hardware

To create a more professional appearance, metal hardware is designed into most of these bags. This hardware can give your creation a unique pop. Each pattern has a list of hardware required. Hardware kits for these bags are available to make sourcing the hardware easy. See Resources on page 170 for more information.

Not all of the bags require hardware. No hardware is needed for the *Clear-as-Day Tote* (page 116), and the hardware can be completely omitted on the *Double-Take Clutch* (page 94). Three more bags—the *Lunch Date Clutch* (page 82), *Free-Spirit Drawstring Purse* (page 44) and *Piccadilly Purse* (page 54)—can be made with some of the hardware omitted.

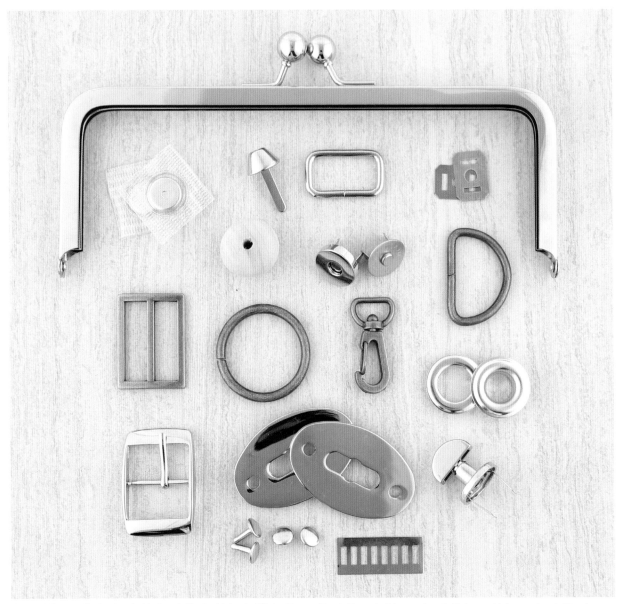

Purse Frame, Twist Lock Unit set, Swivel Hook, Slide, Purse Feet, Sew-In Magnet set, External Magnet set, Rectangle, O-Ring, D-Ring, Bead, Eyelet set, and Center Post Buckle

Terms

To help you understand the terminology, here is an abbreviated list of terms used in this book with their definitions.

Backstitching: Stitching in reverse with the sewing machine to secure the seam.

Baste: Sew a long machine stitch length, or hand stitch. This usually holds something in place temporarily.

Bias: Bias/diagonal cut. The grain of a fabric runs in the direction of the selvage. The bias is 45 degrees from that selvage. With cotton there is usually no stretch on the grain, but there is stretch when pulling the fabric 45 degrees from the grain. Cutting binding on the bias is helpful in places that might need a little give or stretch to smoothly reach around an area, especially a curve. (See page 15 for more on cutting bias binding.)

Blindstitch: Small, hidden hand stitches.

Ease: This describes the even distribution of slight fullness when one section of a seam is joined to a slightly shorter section without forming gathers or tucks.

Edge stitch: Topstitch ⅛" (3mm) using a seam, edge or fold as a guide.

Finish seam: Serge or zigzag along the cut raw edge to prevent fraying.

Gathering stitches: Using a long stitch length, sew at ⅜" (1cm) from the raw edge and again ⅜" (1cm) from the previous stitching. Lines run parallel to each other. Pull the top threads to adjust the gathers between marks.

Overlay: A piece that is placed over another in the finished product.

Right side: The pretty side that is seen when the project is done.

Right sides facing: The right sides of two fabrics are facing each other or are against each other.

Right-side out: The right side of the fabric is facing outward.

Right and left: As pieces appear when placed on the workspace with the right side up.

Seam allowance: The area between the raw edge and the stitching.

Satin stitch: A very tight zigzag machine stitch that doesn't travel, but stays stationary.

Stitch in the ditch: Topstitch along a seam, using the line between the two fabrics as a guide.

Tack (down): Make several small stitches by hand or machine in one place to invisibly secure.

Topstitch: On the right side, stitch ¼" or ⅜" (6mm or 1cm) away from the edge, seam or previous stitching, as directed. The stitch is both decorative and functional.

Wrong side: The back of the fabric.

Wrong sides facing: The back sides, or wrong sides, of two fabrics are facing each other or are against each other.

Wrong-side out: The back side, or wrong side, of the fabric is facing outward.

Whipstitch: A stitch made by hand or by machine that works back and forth several times in the same place to secure layers of fabric together or create a secured stopping point, like at the end of a zipper that has been cut. If the intent of the stitch is to bind the raw edges of multiple pieces of fabric together to protect against unraveling, the back-and-forth stitches will progress gradually around the edges, going through and over the edge of the fabric.

Special Techniques

Signature Bags focuses on unique designs and is not meant to teach you how to sew. With that said, my intent in including all the tips is to assist my sewers in creating a positive experience and to make steps easier and quicker, resulting in a more professional-looking bag. These are not inclusive, basic instructions on each subject, but instead build upon a basic knowledge of the subject. Some explain techniques that may be unfamiliar to the hobby sewer.

Cutting Fabric

Some of these bags have many pieces. Label the pieces as you cut them. Measurements are expressed as width by length. Press and starch all fabrics flat prior to fine-tuning cuts. When measuring and cutting, use a cutting mat with lines. Always double-check measurements before cutting. But don't expect perfection. Refine cuts after fusing because, sometimes, fabric stretches during this process.

Pressing Fabric

Press often. Press and starch all the pieces before sewing because it is usually impossible to press folds out of fabric pieces once the bag is finished. A fully pressed bag is more professional looking. A good press can also remove some pin marks. Hint: When pressing a pocket that has been sewn on all sides and then turned right side out, lay the piece so the seams are centered. Press the seams flat with only the tip of the iron. Then, when the pocket is folded with the seams on the edge, it will more fully extend to a square shape. Pressing flat at this point will produce straighter lines.

Topstitching

When topstitching, leave the needle in the down position when turning a corner. After turning the corner but before lifting the needle and moving forward, check that no pressure is pulling the needle out of the centered position.

Avoid backstitching. This is possible when the stitching is cosmetic. When attaching two separate pieces, however, backstitching might be necessary. One trick to avoid backstitching is to pull the top thread of the last stitch through to the back side by pulling the bobbin thread a little. Then tie the top and bobbin threads into a knot. Alternately, when topstitching a continuous line where you end at the same place you began the stitching, simply overlap the topstitching lines by four or five stitches.

For long, straight edges, especially down the middle of an open space, put masking tape along the topstitching line to provide a guide to keep the stitching straight.

Remove pins before sewing over them, as they can shift the foot a little, creating a buckle in the line or an unevenness in the stitch length.

To avoid tail ends of thread showing on the outside of a piece, clip the top thread first. Pull the bobbin thread slightly, and it will pull the last stich from the front to the back.

Sewing and Clipping Curves

If you have a tendency to sew curves a little "off," draw the seam with a pencil on the wrong side first. Sew the seam with a stitch length of about 1.5 around the curves. The smaller stitch allows for a smoother look when the piece is turned right-side out.

While making clips into the seam allowance is the best way to help ease a seam when you align a curved edge with a straight edge, a curved seam that will be turned right-side out is treated differently. Instead, simply trim that seam allowance to ⅛" (3mm) without making the tiny clips. This makes the finished curve smoother.

Finishing the Lining

One of the final stages of bag construction is often closing the lining layer that was left open to facilitate turning everything right-side out. The sewer is usually instructed to topstitch the opening closed. In these cases, choose between topstitching or blindstitching. Topstitching by machine is more noticeable on the inside of the bag, but it is secure. Blindstitching by hand can be almost invisible, but the threads break more easily with this stitch. Choose your preference.

Cutting Bias Binding

- Fold one corner of fabric to the opposite corner. (Fig. A)
- Cut strips of fabric to the width indicated in the cutting instructions. (Fig. B)
- Piece the strips together at an angle as shown. (Fig. C and D)

Turning Narrow Pieces Right-Side Out

Turning a narrow piece right-side out can be tedious. Try attaching a safety pin to the end of the tube of fabric and thread it through the inside, as if you were guiding elastic through a casing. If the end is closed, you can position a narrow stick, like the flat end of a barbecue skewer, at that end and pull the rest of the fabric down over the stick.

Working with Peltex

Peltex is used for strong support in these bags. Exercise a little caution when sewing with Peltex because it can lose its strength and shape when bent. Due to the unique quality of this product, some instructions have been adapted so the

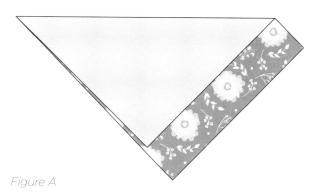

Figure A

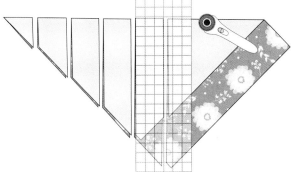

Figure B

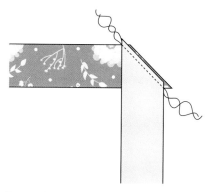

Figure C

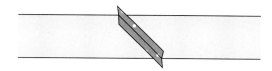

Figure D

Peltex is inserted at the end, after the bag has already been turned right-side out. Turning any of the bags right-side out can stress the supporting layers, especially Peltex layers. Take your time and be gentle during this process.

Sewing Laminated Cotton and Clear Vinyl

Laminated cotton wipes off easily, but be cautious as it is not waterproof. Liquids left for a length of time on the fabric can seep under the coating, making it impossible to clean. Clear vinyl comes in many thicknesses. All of these products sew and respond to heat differently. Experiment with several techniques on each product before diving in or getting frustrated.

Pressing: Only press if necessary. Over-pressing takes away some of the finish on the laminate. While working with clear vinyl, keep it flat. Wrinkling or folding clear vinyl may leave marks in the material; this is less the case with laminate. Some creases can be remedied by heating with an iron on a warm setting through a press cloth. Leave a freshly pressed laminate or clear vinyl piece untouched until it is fully cooled. Test a piece first before attempting to press. If left near heat, either material could melt.

Fusing: Place the fabric right-side down. Place the fusible fleece/woven fusible interfacing with the shiny adhesive-side down over the fabric. Cover it with a pressing cloth. With your iron at the wool/steam setting, slowly iron the fabric in place. Use a pressing action for fusible fleece and a gliding action for woven fusible interfacing,

If fusing laminate, note that heat will penetrate through the stabilizers more easily than the laminate. Continually check the laminate to make sure the surface isn't getting too warm. After fusing fusible fleece to the wrong side of the laminate, let it cool completely before moving the piece. Because you are fusing through some thickness, you'll need steam to ensure solid adhesion.

Combating the Drag: Laminate and clear vinyl have a tendency to create a drag on the sewing machine. Each machine works through the drag differently. Where there is a little drag, put transparent tape on the presser foot. Leave a small gap for the needle to go through. Also, put some tape along the bottom plate of the sewing machine next to the feed dogs (or the riveted metal parts that move the fabric). But don't cover up the feed dogs.

Another method is to apply a drop of sewing machine oil on the presser foot by rubbing a little on it with your finger. Of course, the oil shouldn't get on any cotton, but it can be easily wiped off laminate or clear vinyl. Always try it on a small piece first, and wipe the oil off immediately. A third option is to invest in a Teflon presser foot or walking foot.

Aside from making adjustments with the sewing machine, a few other things can be done to work through the unusual feel of sewing on vinyl products. Where possible, sew seams with the cotton layer, if there is a cotton layer, on top of the laminate (or clear vinyl) layer. Also, when top-stitching, use a slightly longer stitch (3 to 3.5).

Pinning: When a pin pierces clear vinyl, it leaves a permanent hole. Therefore, pin only in the seam allowance where it will be covered, or pin exactly where the sewing machine stitches will be. Use silk pins to minimize the size of the holes.

Fabric Protection: If applying fabric protection on the cotton areas of a bag that has clear vinyl as well, like the *Clear-as-Day Tote* (page 116), spray the fabric protection on the cotton pieces before constructing the bag. The spray can cloud the clear vinyl surfaces.

Repurposing Denim Jeans

Reusing old jeans can be creative and economical. It takes a little extra work and a lot of creativity. The goal is to make your project look like the denim was originally made for it.

Topstitching: Topstitch pieces of denim from the same pair of jeans together to achieve the size needed. Copy the thread color and topstitching style that is in the original denim.

Use Detail: Use all the original jean detail possible, and create a way for the denim areas to lay flat. For example, long straps can be cut from the legs of jeans using the inseam topstitching as an accent down the center of the strap. Or unpick belt loops and reattach in unexpected locations. The waistband has straight edges with a great button or snap for an accent. Manipulate the crotch so it lies flat, tuck loose fabric under, and then topstitch over the original topstitching of the crotch. (Note: Not all pieces can be made flat.) These techniques can look natural and become part of a bigger piece.

Piecing: To create a long strip, use the fly from the waistband down to slightly below the zipper topstitching. Piece the rest of the strip using a side front pocket and some flat pieces. (Fig. E)

Adapting the Pattern: If the plan is to topstitch something like a waistband in an area that calls for a seam, take away the amount of the seam allowance from the cut piece. Most patterns try to hide seams, but sometimes exposed seams create a unique accent. For example, the shoulder straps are usually folded seam against seam. Try flipping the seam to the outside.

Distressed Areas: Holes in denim can be a fantastic accent. Cut a spare piece of denim 2" (5cm) bigger than the hole and in the same shade. On the wrong side of the denim, apply fabric glue all around the hole. Press the patch piece against the glue. The right side of the denim patch might show through the hole. Put weight on it for a couple of hours. You can finish here, or for more

detail, sew long crisscrossed lines on the surface. Sew the lines unevenly in length and slightly close to each other. Overshoot the hole so the topstitching looks original and intentional. Don't cut away fraying and loose threads from the original hole. Simply sew over the loose threads, laying them in the direction they originally went.

Pocket: If incorporating a pocket as a focal point, cut the pocket or flap with an additional ½" (1.3cm) or more all around. Tuck the excess ½" (1.3cm) under with the wrong side facing so only the pocket is exposed with no raw edges. Topstitch the perimeter using the existing topstitching lines as a guide. Don't unpick pockets from the original garments because it is likely great topstitching will be removed. Front pockets are best if sewn closed with the inside pocket fabric cut away. Embroidered or studded pockets are fantastic. If the pocket is narrower than what the pattern requires, cut your piece around the pocket larger to make up for the difference, and then be consistent with the rest of the perimeter of the pocket.

Keep in Mind: Worn denim has some give or stretch. Using stretch denim will not work. Be consistent with the grain of the fabric when cutting pieces and when piecing bigger pieces.

Your Machine: Before jumping in, practice to see how many layers of denim your sewing machine can work through. Keep that in mind as you begin piecing layers on top of each other.

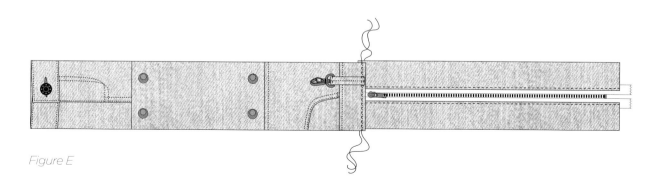

Figure E

Installing Hardware

Installing a Magnetic Snap Set (exterior application): Push the prongs of the magnetic snap into the fabric hard enough to leave indentations in the fabric where it will be installed. Use a craft knife or seam ripper to cut small slits at the indentations, through all layers of material. Do the same with a 1" (2.5cm) square of Peltex. Push the prongs through the slits from the right side. From the wrong side, thread Peltex onto the prongs and then the washer. Flatten the prongs outward, using a screwdriver, if needed, to push down the prongs, pinching the fabric tightly to hold the snap in place. (Fig. F)

Installing a Magnetic Snap Set (sew-in application): To give added integrity to the vinyl covering the magnets, place a 1½" (3.8cm) piece of cotton over the magnet so it is sandwiched between two pieces of cotton when topstitched in place.

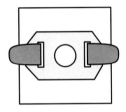

Figure F

Installing Purse Feet: Using a craft knife or seam ripper, cut a slit through all layers at the location indicated for installation. Slide the prongs through the slit from the right side and flatten outward on the wrong side of the bag. Use a screwdriver, if needed, to push down the prongs. Push the prongs firmly to hold the feet in place.

Gluing into Purse Frames: Open the purse frame. Run a continuous bead of glue in the groove of the front half of the frame. Quickly get the edges of the purse approximately in place to stop the possibility of dripping, then fine-tune the position all along the edge. Use a screwdriver or table knife to help tuck the fabric all the way into the groove. All edges must be all the way to the top of the groove for an even line and solid adhesion. Keep the center of the bag lined up with the center of the frame. The fabric may creep out as you work along the edge. To help keep the fabric in position as you move along, tape the fabric and the frame together every couple of inches (centimeters). Once in place, pull the sides by the frame joint out a little and add additional glue. Repeat for the back edge of the frame.

Check to see that any glue seeping out gets cleaned away from the fabric and frame immediately. After 24 hours, check the adhesion. If some parts are coming out (which they often do), slip a little glue into those places and give it a day to dry.

Small clutches are not made to hold heavy things. To add support, use needle-nose pliers to squeeze the frame edges together. Place a thick piece of fabric between the frame and the pliers to protect the finish on the frame.

Installing Eyelets/Grommets: Cut the hole exactly the size of the opening. If the fabric is stretched a little, it makes a bulge in the fabric once the eyelet is installed. If installing through several layers, especially if there are ruffles, whipstitch the eyelet hole through all the layers. From the right side, insert the ridged half of the eyelet through all the layers of fabric. From the opposite side of the fabric, place the other half of the eyelet/grommet over the first. Squeeze in place with pliers or hammer in place with a post tool.

Installing a Twist Lock (stationary half): The pieces you'll need are one face plate with ridge, one flat back plate, two posts and two post ends. The stationary half of the lock should be installed through two layers of fabric with a number of stabilizing products between them. Have all these layers lined up in finished position. Place the face plate of the twist lock where you want it to be located, and trace around the opening for the hole. Mark the location of the posts as well. Using embroidery scissors with sharp tips, cut out the hole, making it large enough so the fabric will not buckle when both pieces are in place, but not too large. Also cut holes where the posts will go through. (Fig. G)

Figure G

Figure H

With a tiny stitch length on your machine, topstitch around the opening or whipstitch by hand. You could apply a little adhesive onto both sides of the metal pieces. Place both plates over the hole: the face plate on the front and the back plate behind. Squeeze together, making sure they are perfectly straight. From the front, insert a post through to the back. Place a drop of glue on the post end and align it with the post. Working on a hard surface with something to protect the finish of the lock plate, place the plate front-side down. Put a folded piece of fabric over the post end to protect the finish. Hammer the post end for a firm connection with the post. Do the same with the other post and post end.

Installing a Twist Lock (twisting half): The pieces you'll need are one turn piece and one washer. Align the stationary half of the lock over the place where the twisting half will be to double-check placement. (Fig. H)

Push the prongs of the lock into the fabric hard enough to make indentations in the fabric. (Fig. I)

Use a craft knife or seam ripper to cut slits at the indentations, through all the layers of material. Do the same with a 4" (10cm) square of Peltex. Push the prongs through the slits from the right side of the fabric. From the wrong side, thread on the Peltex piece and then the washer. Flatten the prongs outward, using a screwdriver, if needed, to push the prongs. Pinch the fabric tightly to hold the snap in place. (Fig. J)

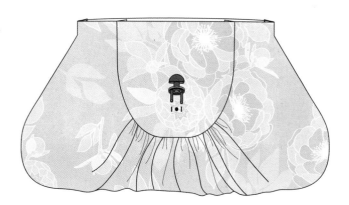

Figure I

Figure J

CHAPTER ONE

Purses and Clutches

Ruffles, buckles, magnets, piping, metal hardware, surprising handles and adjustable straps are just a few of the features you will enjoy sewing in these purses, clutches and wallet.

A unique quality is offered in each design. The clutches can be your all-day, everyday solution for convenience. Hang either of these clutch designs over your shoulder, and you will have everything you need at your fingertips. The wallet is small enough to fit into your purse, but fulfills every wallet need.

Sewing with laminated cotton or clear vinyl might be a new experience, but you will be impressed with the results. There is no need for handmade accessories to look hastily homemade. Let any of these purses reflect your sense of style and attitude toward life. Take the leap.

Park Bench Ruffle Purse

The *Park Bench Ruffle Purse* is not for the shy lady—you will get a lot of attention when holding this purse layered with ruffles and dotted with oversized covered buttons. The ruffles are gathered on the over-the-shoulder straps. Piece the ruffles with your favorite scraps to liven up the look. Inside this roomy purse, you will find a mobile phone pocket and a zippered pocket. Go ahead—make your flirty fashion statement with enthusiasm.

Size

16" wide × 11" tall × 6" deep
(40.5cm × 28cm × 15cm)

Level of Difficulty (intermediate)

Fabric Choices

Everything is lightweight about this purse. Quilting cotton is preferred. Home décor weight fabric will work for the overlay of the purse, but do not reinforce it with woven fusible interfacing. Soft and Stable is best for the stability of the purse. If you substitute fusible fleece for the Soft and Stable, the bag will not be strong enough to stand independently.

Skills to Review

Installing a Magnetic Snap Set
   (exterior application) (page 18)
Sewing and Clipping Curves (page 14)
Topstitching (page 14)
Turning Narrow Pieces Right-Side Out (page 15)
Working with Peltex (page 15)

Materials

Yardage

1 yard (91.5cm) accent fabric for ruffles

½ yard (45.5cm) exterior or alternate fabric for overlay

⅓ yard (30.5cm) accent fabric for handles and tabs

⅔ yard (61cm) fabric for exterior

1¼ yards (1.1m) fabric for lining

1 yard (91.5m) woven fusible interfacing, 20" (51cm) wide

12" × 18" (30.5cm × 45.5cm) piece of Peltex

18" × 40" (45.5cm × 101.5cm) piece of Soft and Stable

Hardware

4 O-rings, 1¼" (3.2cm)

1 set of exterior magnets

3 button forms for covering, 1⅛" (2.9cm)

Notions

1 zipper, 7" (18cm)

43" (109cm) piping cord, ²²⁄₃₂" (1.7cm)

5 yards (4.6m) ruffle lace, 2" (5cm), if using lace instead of pieced ruffle

Patterns

Park Bench Ruffle Purse patterns: Bottom, Overlay (on CD)

Featured fabric by Lila Tueller of Lila Tueller Designs

Cutting

> Note: Measurements are given as width × length. See cutting charts on the CD, if desired.

From exterior fabric, cut:
1 aa strip 2½" × 34" (6.5cm × 86.5cm) for Body Strips
5 bb strips 2" × 34" (5cm × 86.5cm) for Body Strips
1 cc strip 5½" × 34" (14cm × 86.5cm) for Body Strips
1 Bottom from pattern
1 Overlay from pattern

From accent fabric, cut:
4 A strips 4" × 70" (10cm × 178cm) for Ruffle Strips*
1 B strip 4" × 22" (10cm × 56cm) for Ruffle Strips*
1 C strip 4" × 13" (10cm × 33cm) for Ruffle Strips*
1 rectangle 3¼" × 16" (8.5cm × 40.5cm) for Tabs
2 rectangles 3" × 45" (7.5cm × 114.5cm) for Handles

From lining fabric, cut:
1 rectangle 33" × 11½" (84cm × 29cm) for Lining
1 rectangle 9" × 6" (23cm × 15cm) for Flat Pocket
1 rectangle 9¼" × 10" (23.5cm × 25.5cm) for Zipper
   Pocket
1 Bottom from pattern
1 Overlay from pattern

From woven fusible interfacing, cut:
1 rectangle 3¼" × 16" (8.5cm × 40.5cm) for Tabs
1 Bottom from pattern
1 Overlay from pattern

From Peltex, cut:
2 Bottom pieces from pattern

From Soft and Stable, cut:
1 aa strip 2½" × 34" (6.5cm × 86.5cm) for Body Strips
5 bb strips 2" × 34" (5cm × 86.5cm) Body Strips
1 cc strip 5½" × 34" (14cm × 86.5cm) Body Strips
1 Bottom from pattern

*If using 2" (5cm) Ruffle Lace instead of Ruffle Strips, cut:
4 A strips 35" (89cm) long
1 B strip 11" (28cm) long
1 C strip 6" (15cm) long

Tips on Ruffles

This pattern calls for long 4" (10cm) strips. These can be from one fabric or pieced from many fabrics (see below). You can also use 2" (5cm) trim. The scalloped edge of a lace can be used if 2" (5cm) is trimmed off the bottom edge. For both 2" (5cm) options, do not fold in half lengthwise. The lace or trim will have exposed raw edges at the seam allowance where the ends are connected to make long strips. Serge, zigzag stitch or use pinking shears to finish or hide raw edges. Adjust strips so this seam is hidden in the back of the bag. On short ruffles (B) and (C), fold ends twice at ¼" (6mm) with wrong sides facing and topstitch at ⅛" (3mm) to finish the edge. Keep these tips in mind because the instructions and illustrations are for cotton ruffles.

Tips on Piecing Strips

The pieces in the pieced strips do not have to be even in length. The lengths can be 2"–8" (5cm–20.5cm) long, so use all of your favorite scraps. Sew pieces with ¼" (6mm) seam allowance. Press pieces well before cutting and after sewing. You may choose to topstitch the seams to one side. This is more of a country look and can be really cute. Once something has been ruffled, it's almost impossible to press the fabric well, so take the opportunity to press here. After connecting the 70" (178cm) strip into a loop and pressing it in half lengthwise, determine which pieced sections you want in the front. (The front has the most exposed sections of ruffles.) Determine the front and back of the pieced strip and sew the gathering stitches accordingly.

Preparing Pieces

1 Trim ¼" (6mm) from the perimeter of the Bottom Lining and ⅝" (1.5cm) off the Bottom Peltex pieces.

2 According to the manufacturer's instructions, fuse woven fusible interfacing to the wrong side of the Tabs, Bottom Exterior and Overlay Accent.

3 Pin Soft and Stable to the wrong side of the related Body Strip pieces and Bottom Exterior. Pull fabric tight over Soft and Stable.

4 Center both Peltex pieces to the Bottom Exterior. Topstitch around the Peltex at ⅛" (3mm).

Ruffle Body

5 Sew the short ends of all BODY STRIPS together, right sides facing, with a ½" (1.3cm) seam allowance, creating loops. Trim the Soft and Stable in the seam allowance to ⅛" (3mm). Press seams open. (Fig. 1)

6 Sew the two short ends of a RUFFLE STRIP A together, right sides facing, with a ¼" (6mm) seam allowance so you have a continuous loop. Repeat for the other three Ruffle Strips A. Fold the loops in half horizontally, wrong sides facing, and press the fold. (Fig. 2)

7 Fold the short ends of RUFFLES B and C over ¼" (6mm), wrong sides facing, and press. Fold the Ruffles in half lengthwise, wrong sides facing, and press. (Fig. 3)

8 Beginning at the seam for Ruffles A or the edges for Ruffles B and C, sew a continuous gathering stitch ⅜" (1cm) from the raw edge/seam; sew another line ⅝" (1.5cm) from the raw edge/seam (Figs. 2 and 3).

Tip: *There are shortcuts to gathering, but I don't trust that they give the finished look you desire. Just do it the old-fashioned way.*

Figure 1

Figure 2

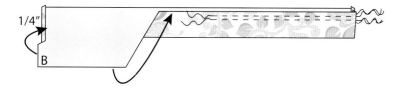

1/4"

Figure 3

9 Align the underside of Ruffle A with right side of Body Strip aa. Align the seams, which will be the back of the Body. Gently pull the pair of top gathering threads of the ruffle strip to evenly arrange the ruffles along the circumference of the Body Strip. Pin in place. Sandwich Ruffle A between Body Strip aa and one Body Strip bb, right sides facing, aligning the seams.

> Tip: Body Strip bb will seem tighter than Body Strip aa because of Soft and Stable thickness. Ease the pieces to fit evenly; when it is turned right-side out, it will fit perfectly.

Sew twice with a ½" (1.3cm) seam allowance. (Fig. 4) Remove gathering stitches. Trim Soft and Stable in the seam allowance to ⅛" (3mm). Turn right-side out. From the right side, topstitch the seam allowance to Body Strip (bb) at ⅛" (3mm). Trim the extra seam allowance away from the wrong side.

10 Repeat step 9 for the remaining Ruffles and Body Strips in the order illustrated. (Fig. 5) Ruffle B will gather in the center front 10" (25.4cm) and Ruffle C will gather in the center front 5" (12.7cm). For Ruffles B and C, topstitch the ends of the ruffle to the Body piece at ⅛" (3mm). (Fig. 6)

Assembling the Body

11 Fold the body in half, bringing the center front and back together, right sides facing. Draw an angled line as illustrated. Sew along the line. Trim the seam allowance to ½" (1.3cm) (see Fig. 7). Trim Soft and Stable out of the seam allowance. Repeat for the other side.

Cut ⅜" (1cm) clips every ½" (1.3cm) along the lower edge of the Bottom Exterior. (Fig. 7)

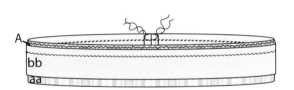

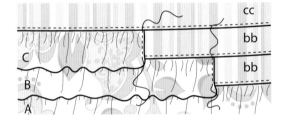

Figure 4

Figure 6

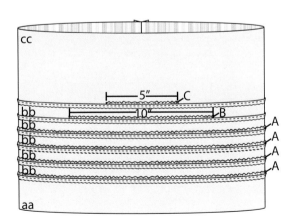

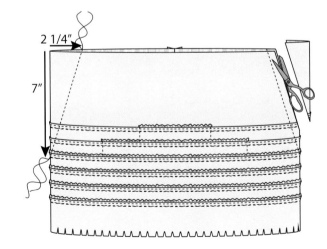

Figure 5

Figure 7

12 Align the center front and back of the Body and BOTTOM pieces, right sides facing. Use the clips in the fabric to evenly ease around the curves. Sew with a ½" (1.3cm) seam allowance, making sure not to catch the bottom ruffle in the seam. (Fig. 8) Trim Soft and Stable in the seam allowance from both pieces to ⅛" (3mm). Turn right-side out.

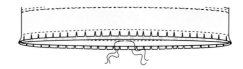

Figure 8

Overlay

13 Align the OVERLAY EXTERIOR and LINING pieces with each other, right sides facing. Sew the outer edge with a ½" (1.3cm) seam allowance and trim to ⅛" (3mm). (Fig. 9) Follow the instruction in Sewing and Clipping Curves on page 14 for sewing and trimming the seam allowance.

14 Press the seam flat with the seam allowance toward the Lining. From the right side, edge stitch the seam allowance to the Lining. Turn right-side out. Press flat.

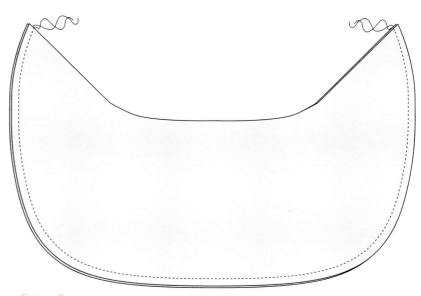

Figure 9

15 Align the raw edge of the Lining Overlay onto the right side of the Body piece. Match the center backs of both pieces and pin around to the front. The side seams of the bag dip a little, so bring the Overlay a little above the dip (about ¼" [6mm]) to make an even line. The left overlay end will overlap the right. The ends are exactly the same distance from the side seam (about 2½" [6.5cm]), ensuring a centered front opening. Baste with a ½" (6mm) seam allowance. (Fig. 10)

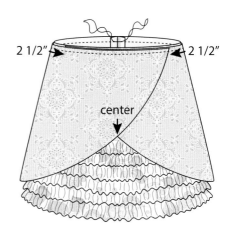

2 1/2"   2 1/2"

center

Figure 10

Handles

16 Fold both ends of one HANDLE piece back ¼" (6mm), wrong sides facing, and press. Fold the Handle piece in half lengthwise, right sides facing. Sew the long seam with a ¼" (6mm) seam allowance. (Fig. 11) Attach a safety pin to one end at the seam. Thread the safety pin into the center of the sewn piece and guide it through to turn the piece right-side out.

> Tip: To give added strength to the ends of the cording prior to threading it into the fabric, I highly recommend sewing a 21½" (54.5cm) piece of ½" (1.3cm) seam tape to the ends of the cording.

17 Sew one end of a 21½" (54.5cm) length of cording at ¼" (6mm) several times for reinforcement. Attach a safety pin to the cording just past the stitching and guide the cording into the Handle piece. (Fig. 12) Gather the extra fullness of the Handle piece in the center area of the cording. Pull the cording through the first end so the fabric extends 1" (2.5cm) beyond the cording. Securely pin so it doesn't come loose. Finish the other end so the fabric extends 1" (2.5cm) beyond the cording. Remove the safety pin from the cording. Pin this end snugly as well.

18 Flatten the ends of the Handle tube so the seam is centered. Thread one end through an O-ring and fold 1" (2.5cm) back on itself, seam against seam. Flatten the end of the cord. Tuck the corners of fabric under to help hide the edges. Topstitch a rectangle to secure. (Fig. 13) Repeat with the other end of the Handle.

19 Repeat steps 16–18 for the remaining Handle.

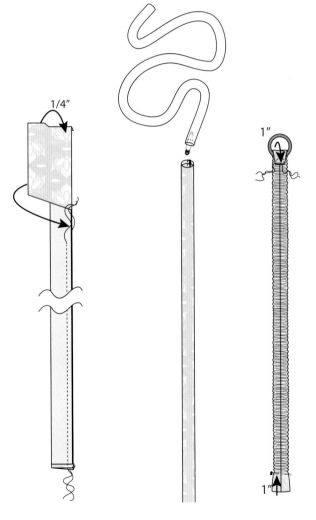

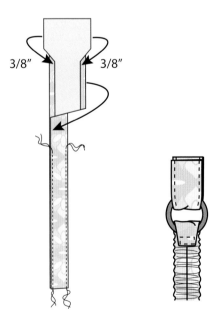

Figure 11   Figure 12   Figure 13   Figure 14   Figure 15

Tabs

20 Press and fold the TABS, wrong sides facing, as illustrated. The finished width is 1¼" (3.2cm). Topstitch both sides at ⅛" (3mm). (Fig. 14)

21 Cut the Tab strip into four pieces of 4" (10cm) each. Slip the raw edge of one Tab through an O-ring on the handle and fold the Tab in half. (Fig. 15) Place the Tab 2½" (6.5cm) from the Body center. Extend the raw edge of the Tab ½" (1.3cm) above the Body raw edge. (Fig. 16) Repeat for all Tabs and O-rings. Baste each Tab in place at ½" (6mm). Turn the Body wrong-side out.

Tip: The front of the Handle, or non-seam side of the Handle, faces away from the purse interior. One Handle attaches to the front of the purse, and the other Handle attaches to the back of the purse.

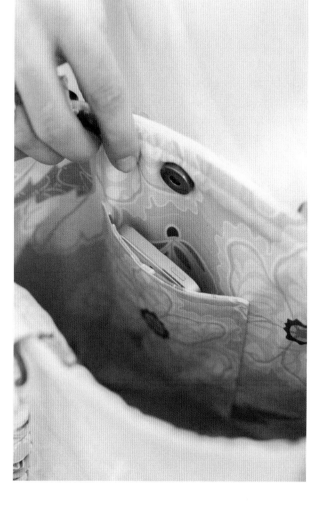

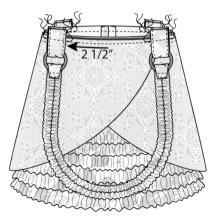

Figure 16

Flat Pocket

22 Bring the short ends of the FLAT POCKET together, right sides facing. Sew with a ½" (1.3cm) seam allowance. Press the seam open. Bring the seam around to the center. Sew the top raw edge with a ½" (1.3cm) seam allowance. This is the top of the pocket. Clip the corners. (Fig. 17) Turn right-side out. Topstitch the top edge at ¼" (6mm). Tuck the raw edges under ½" (1.3cm), wrong sides facing, and pin closed. (Fig. 18)

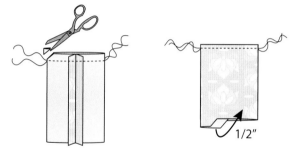

Figure 17   *Figure 18*

23 Position the Pocket back side 2¾" (7cm) down from the top raw edge of the right side of the BODY LINING piece and 6½" (16.5cm) in from the right edge. Topstitch the sides and bottom of the Pocket at ¼" (6mm). (Fig. 19)

Zipper Pocket

24 Place the ZIPPER POCKET piece on top of the left side of the Body Lining piece, as illustrated, right sides facing, with the short end of the pocket up. Draw a 7¼" (18.5cm) long × ½" (1.3cm) high rectangle as illustrated (Fig. 19). Topstitch the rectangle. Cut down the center of the rectangle and out to all four corners at each end, being careful not to clip through stitching. (Fig. 19) Insert Pocket

piece through slit to wrong side of Lining and press around opening, creating a finished window slot. Press the opening flat.

25 Center the zipper on the inside of the Pocket through the opening with the zipper facing out. From the right side, topstitch around the rectangle at ⅛" (3mm) and again at ¼" (6mm), making sure to secure the zipper in place. (Fig. 20)

26 Fold the Pocket fabric in half, right sides facing. Folding the Body Lining piece out of the way, sew the three raw edges of the Pocket with a ¼" (6mm) seam allowance. (Fig. 21)

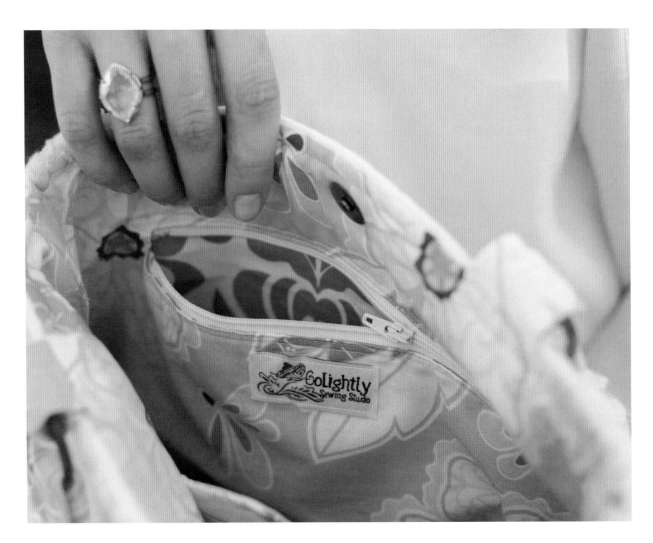

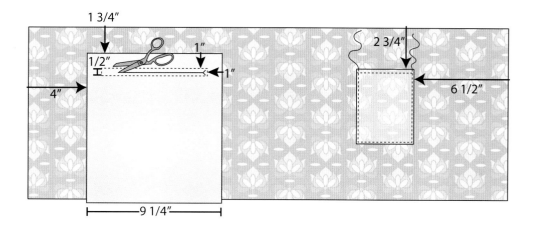

Figure 19

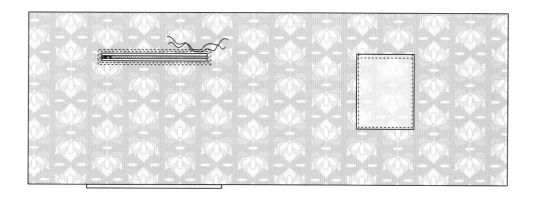

Figure 20

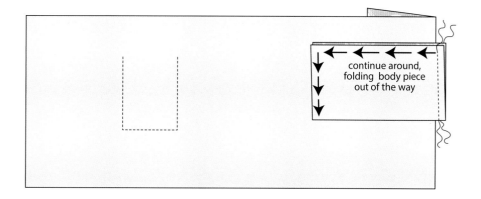

continue around,
folding body piece
out of the way

Figure 21

Assembling the Lining

27 Fold the Lining in half, bringing the short sides together, right sides facing. Draw lines as illustrated. Sew along the lines as illustrated, leaving part of the left-hand seam open for turning. Trim the seam allowance to ½" (1.3cm). (Fig. 22)

28 Cut ⅜" (1cm) clips every ½" (1.3cm) along the lower edge of the Bottom Lining. Align the center front and back of the Body and Bottom pieces, right sides facing. Use the clips in the fabric to evenly ease around the curves.

29 Sew with a ½" (1.3cm) seam allowance. Turn right-side out.

Finishing the Body

30 With the Exterior wrong-side out, tuck the Overlay, Tabs and Handles inside. Set the Lining inside the Exterior, right sides facing. The Lining side that has the zipper pocket will be facing the back of the Exterior. The overhanging raw edges of the Tabs will extend above the Body raw edges.

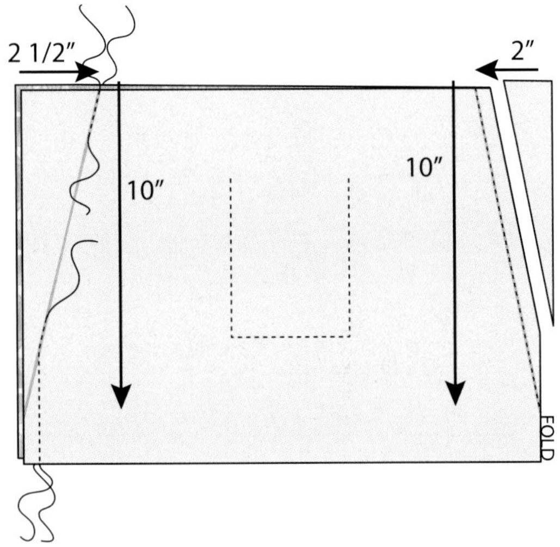

31 Align the center front and back of both pieces. Pin the top raw edges. Slightly ease to fit. Sew the perimeter with a ½" (1.3cm) seam allowance. Backstitch over the Tab areas several times for added reinforcement.

32 Trim the Soft and Stable out of the seam allowance. Turn right-side out through the Lining opening.

33 Working from the Lining side, pull the Tabs, Handles and Overlay out of the way, and top-stitch the top edge of the purse at ⅜" (1cm) through the Exterior and Lining layers, but not the Overlay.

> Tip: Use a strong needle because you are sewing though many layers. Take your time because this stitching is visible in the finished purse when it is opened.

Magnetic Snap

34 Under the Overlay, install the magnetic snaps, centered front and back and ¾" (2cm) down from top edge. Use the opening in the lining to insert a 1" (2.5cm) square piece of Peltex between the Lining and the Soft and Stable layers to reinforce the magnets.

> Tip: The slits and prongs will go through the Exterior, Soft and Stable, and Lining, but not the Overlay. The prongs will be hidden by the Overlay. See page 18 for more on installing magnetic snaps.

35 Topstitch the opening in the Lining closed.

2 1/2"   2"

10"   10"

FOLD

Figure 22

Buttons

36 Cover three buttons according to the manufacturer's instructions. Sew by hand in the locations illustrated. (Fig. 23) Sew through only one layer of the Overlay.

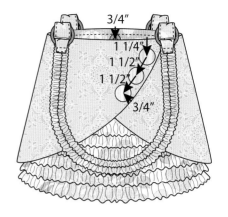

Figure 23

Serendipity Purse

The Serendipity Purse is simultaneously casual and dressy. It is the sort of purse that can bring out the girl in you. The front gathers create a feminine touch, while the twist lock gives a polished look. The unique handles and shape make it truly one-of-a-kind. There are a pair of flat pockets inside as well as a zipper pocket.

Size

15½" wide × 7½" tall × 4" deep
(39.5cm × 19cm × 10cm)

Level of Difficulty (easy)

Fabric Choices

This purse is perfect for quilting cotton fabric. If you choose home décor weight fabric, omit the woven fusible interfacing for the Exterior Body and Bottom pieces. Heavy fabrics are not right for this pattern.

Skills to Review

Installing a Twist Lock (page 18)
Sewing and Clipping Curves (page 14)
Topstitching (page 14)
Turning Narrow Pieces Right-Side Out (page 15)
Working with Peltex (page 15)

Materials

Yardage

¾ yard (68.5cm) fabric for exterior

¾ yard (68.5cm) fabric for lining

1½ yards (1.4m) woven fusible interfacing, 20" (51cm) wide

13" × 13" (33cm × 33cm) piece of Peltex

23" × 30" (58.5cm × 76cm) piece of Soft and Stable

7" × 9" (18cm × 23cm) piece of fusible fleece

Hardware

1 twist lock unit

26 beads, 1" (2.5cm)

28 closed jump rings, 10mm

Notions

1 zipper, 7" (18cm)

Patterns

Serendipity Purse pattern pieces: Front Insert, Front Exterior, Back Exterior, Body Lining, Bottom Exterior, Bottom Lining, Flap (on CD)

Featured fabric by Amanda Herring of The Quilted Fish

Cutting

> Note: Measurements are given as width × length. See cutting charts on the CD, if desired.

From exterior fabric, cut:
2 rectangles 3¾" × 23" (9.5cm × 58.5cm) for Handles
1 Front Exterior from pattern
1 Back Exterior from pattern
1 Front Insert from pattern
1 Bottom Exterior from pattern
2 Flap pieces from pattern

From lining fabric, cut:
2 rectangles 9¼" × 12" (23.5cm × 30.5cm) for Pockets
2 Body Lining pieces from pattern
1 Bottom Lining from pattern

From woven fusible interfacing, cut:
2 rectangles 3¾" × 23" (9.5cm × 58.5cm) for Handles
1 Front Exterior from pattern
1 Back Exterior from pattern
1 Front Insert from pattern
1 Bottom Exterior from pattern
2 Flap pieces from pattern

From Peltex, cut:
3 rectangles 3" × 13" (7.5cm × 33cm) for Bottom Exterior
1 rectangle 4" × 4" (10cm × 10cm) for lock support on Body piece

From Soft and Stable, cut:
1 rectangle 3" × 2" (7.5cm × 5cm) for lock support on Flap piece
2 Back Exterior pieces from pattern
1 Bottom Exterior from pattern

From fusible fleece, cut:
1 Flap from pattern

Preparing the Pieces

1 According to the manufacturer's instructions, fuse woven fusible interfacing to the wrong side of the Front Exterior, Back Exterior, Bottom Exterior, Front Insert, Handles and both Flap pieces.

2 Pin Soft and Stable to the wrong side of the related Back Exterior piece and Bottom Exterior piece. Pull the fabric snugly over the Soft and Stable.

3 According to the manufacturer's instructions, fuse fusible fleece to the wrong side of one Flap piece.

Front Body

4 Cut ⅜" (1cm) clips along the inner curved edge of the FRONT EXTERIOR.

5 Sew a pair of gathering stitches between the dots along the bottom and top of the Front Exterior Front piece. (Fig. 1)

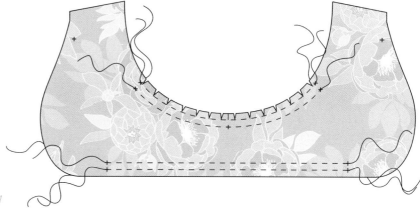

Figure 1

6 Align the FRONT INSERT piece curved edges with the Front Exterior piece, right sides facing. Use the clips to ease around the curves. Align the middle points and marks on the Front Insert and Front Exterior pieces. Pull the gathering stitches to fit the Front Insert piece.

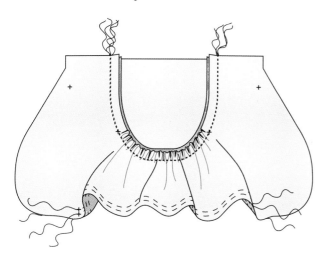

Figure 2

7 Using a small stitch length, sew the curved edge of the Front Insert piece with a ½" (1.3cm) seam allowance. Sew twice. Pull the gathering stitches out. Press the seam allowance toward the Insert. (Fig. 2)

8 Align the remaining piece of Soft and Stable cut from the Back Exterior pattern to the wrong side of this front piece. Pin along the sides and top. Pull the gathering stitches along the bottom so they are arranged evenly on the Soft and Stable. Pull the fabric snug over the Soft and Stable. Pin along the bottom.

Bottom

9 Stack and center the three BOTTOM PELTEX pieces on the wrong side of the BOTTOM EXTE-RIOR piece. From the wrong side, topstitch a rectangle ⅛" (3mm) away from the edge of the Peltex stack.

10 Cut ⅜" (1cm) clips every ½" (1.3cm) along the long curved edges of the Bottom Piece as shown. (Fig. 3)

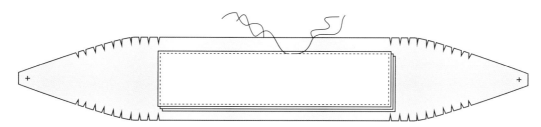

Figure 3

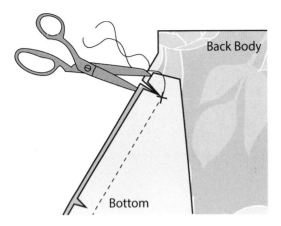

Figure 4

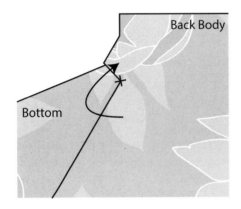

Figure 5

Assembling Exterior Body

11 Align the centers of the Bottom piece and the BACK EXTERIOR piece, right sides facing. Pin two pieces together around the bottom and sides of the Back Exterior piece. Use the clips to evenly ease around curves. Toward the top of the sides, align the mark on the Bottom piece with the mark on the Back Exterior piece. Sew with a ½" (1.3cm) seam allowance from one mark to the other mark. Cut a clip from the raw edge to the mark through both layers and on both sides of the Back Exterior piece. (Fig. 4) Use these clips to move the raw edge of the Bottom piece into the position that will create a continuous line with the Exterior piece. (Fig. 5)

12 Repeat with the other side and Front Body piece. At the top of the sides, align the Front and Back Body pieces, right sides facing. Sew with a ½" (1.3cm) seam allowance. This time sew all the way to the top raw edges. Make sure the new stitches go over the beginning and ending stitches from step 11. (Fig. 6)

13 Trim Soft and Stable in the seam allowance to ⅛" (3mm). Trim the top ⅝" (1.5cm) of Soft and Stable off both Front and Back pieces. Hand baste the Soft and Stable in place. Turn right-side out. Remove the gathering stitches on the Front Exterior piece.

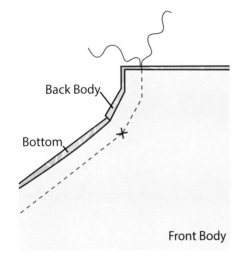

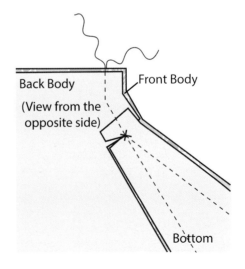

Figure 6

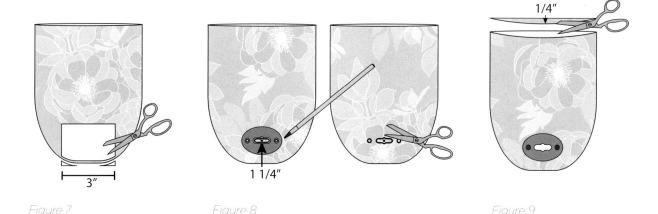

Figure 7   Figure 8   Figure 9

Flap

14 Align both FLAP pieces, right sides facing. Sew along two sides and the curved end with a ½" (1.3cm) seam allowance.

> Tip: Turn the machine stitch length down to 1.5. Tiny stitches help the curve to be smoother.

15 Trim the seam allowance to ⅛" (3mm). Turn right-side out through the unsewn end. Press flat.

Twist Lock

16 Trim the 3" (7.5cm) end of the Soft and Stable piece to match the Flap curve. (Fig. 7) Center the Soft and Stable between the layers. Draw a mark centered and up 1¼" (3.2cm) from the curve of the Flap on the right side. The layer that has the fusible fleece will be the outside of the Flap. Install the stationary half of the lock at this mark. (Fig. 8)

> Tip: See Installing a Twist Lock (stationary half) on page 18 for full instructions.

17 Make a mark ¼" (6mm) down from the center of the raw edge of the inside Flap. Trim an arch on this raw edge with the mark as the lowest point, as illustrated. (Fig. 9)

18 Align the raw edges of the Flap and baste with a ½" (1.3cm) seam allowance.

> Tip: There will be fullness now that the under edge has been trimmed, but this helps the Flap lay flat when the purse is closed.

19 Align the Flap over the right side of the Front Insert. Draw a mark on the Insert, centered in the Twist Lock opening. (Fig. 10)

Figure 10

Figure 11

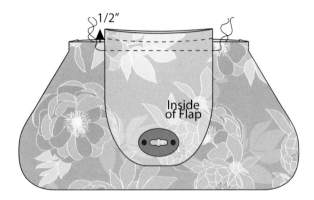

Figure 13

Figure 12

20 Install the twisting half of the lock at this mark. (Fig. 11 and 12)

> Tip: See Installing a Twist Lock (twisting half) on page 18 for full instructions.

21 Center the outside layers of the Flap with the Back Body piece. Extend the Flap raw edge ½" (1.3cm) beyond the Body raw edge. From the Body side, baste the Flap in place ½" (1.3cm) from the Body raw edge. (Fig. 13)

Handles

22 Fold one HANDLE piece in half, bringing the long sides together, right sides facing. Sew with a ¼" (6mm) seam allowance.

23 Turn right-side out by attaching a safety pin to one end and threading it through the center of the fabric.

24 Thread the fabric tube through a jump ring, leaving 1½" (3.8cm) of fabric at the end. Slide a bead into the tube. Pull the fabric snug. (Fig. 14) Repeat until there are 13 beads in the tube and 14 rings on the tube. The tube of fabric will begin and end with a jump ring and 1½" (3.8cm) of extra fabric. If there is more than 1½" (3.8cm) of fabric, cut off the extra. Put a pin near the beginning and ending jump rings to keep the beads tight. Don't remove these pins until the purse is complete.

25 Flatten the raw ends of the Handle tube so the seam is centered.

26 Repeat for the other Handle. If the end was trimmed in step 24, make an identical cut on this Handle.

Figure 14

27 Align the raw ends of the Handles with the top raw edges of the Front Exterior and Back Exterior pieces as illustrated. The raw edge of the Handles will extend ½" (1.3cm) beyond the top of purse. Baste with a ¼" (6mm) seam allowance. (Fig. 15)

Tip: With the Handles hanging down, the seams will face outward. One Handle is on the Front Exterior piece, and the other is on the Back Exterior piece.

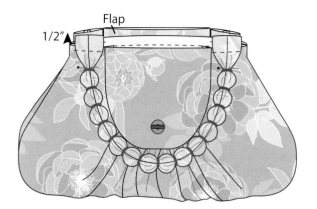

Figure 15

Flat Lining Pocket

28 Bring the short ends of one POCKET rectangle together, right sides facing. Sew around the sides and bottom with a ¼" (6mm) seam allowance, leaving a 3" (7.5cm) opening at the bottom for turning. (Fig. 16)

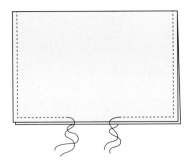

Figure 16

29 Clip the corners. Turn right-side out. Pin the opening closed. Topstitch along the fold at ¼" (6mm). (Fig. 17)

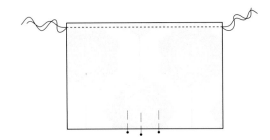

Figure 17

30 Fold the Pocket in half, side to side, and press. This pressed fold will be the guide for topstitching between the pockets.

31 Center the Pocket on the right side of one BODY LINING piece 1¾" (4.5cm) down from the top edge. From the right side, topstitch the two sides, bottom, and on each side of the creased line at ⅛" (3mm). This will close the opening at the bottom and create pocket divisions. (Fig. 18)

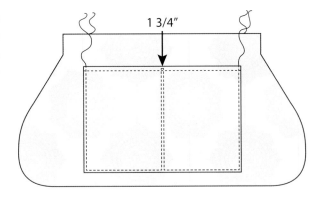

1 3/4"

Figure 18

Zipper Lining Pocket

32 Align the remaining POCKET rectangle short side with the remaining Body Lining piece, right sides facing. Place the Pocket centered and 1" (2.5cm) down from the top of the Lining. Draw a rectangle 7¼" × ½" (18.5cm × 1.3cm) on the wrong side of the Pocket as shown. (Fig. 19) Topstitch this drawn rectangle. Cut down the center of the sewn rectangle and into each corner. Insert the Pocket piece through the slit to the wrong side of Lining and press around the opening, creating a finished window slot.

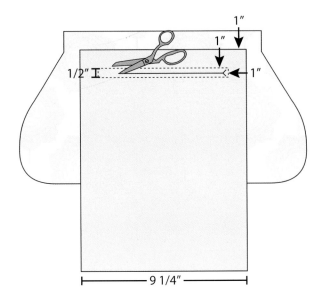

1"

1"

1/2" I

1"

9 1/4"

Figure 19

33 Center the zipper in this opening. From the right side of the Lining, topstitch at ⅛" (3mm) and ¼" (6mm). (Fig. 20)

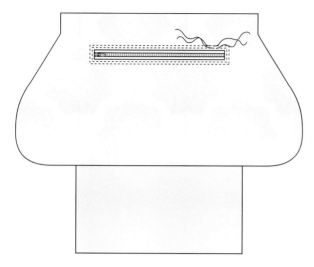

Figure 20

34 Fold the Pocket fabric in half, right sides facing. Moving the Lining out of the way, sew the three raw edges of the Pocket with a ½" (1.3cm) seam allowance. (Fig. 21)

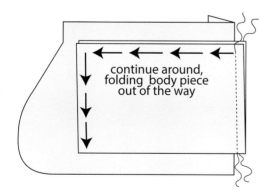

continue around, folding body piece out of the way

Figure 21

Assembling the Lining Body

35 Repeat steps 10–12 to assemble the Body Lining and Bottom Lining pieces. The only difference is that you will leave an 11" (28cm) opening at the bottom for turning. Do not turn right-side out yet.

Finishing

36 Set the Exterior inside the Lining, right sides facing, to match the diagram. (Fig. 22) Tuck the Flap and the Handles inside. The overhanging raw edges of the Flap and the ends of the Handles will extend above the Body raw edges. Align the center front and back of both pieces. Ease slightly, as needed.

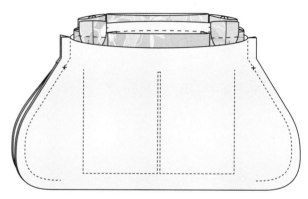

Figure 22

37 Using the zipper foot, sew around the top raw edge with a ½" (1.3cm) seam allowance twice for added support.

Tip: The zipper foot will allow you to sew close to the beads on the Handles and keep them snug. This is the trickiest part of the purse. Because of the many layers and close position of beads, the stitching takes patience.

38 Turn right-side out through the Lining opening. Topstitch the opening closed. Remove the hand basting that held the Soft and Stable in place at the tops of the Back and Front Exterior pieces and the pins holding the handle beads tight.

Free-Spirit Drawstring Purse

Have fancy fashion fun with the *Free-Spirit Drawstring Purse*. The ridiculous volume of ruffles creates a unique focal point for an outfit. For a more traditional woman, leave off the ruffles for a darling shaped purse. The drawstring cinches the top closed, causing the purse to look smaller than it really is. This purse includes an interior pocket, accent piping and an across-the-body strap that adjusts with a 1" (2.5cm) buckle. Choose between the smallish and larger sizes. With this purse you can feel young and sophisticated at the same time.

Size

Smallish: 6½" wide × 8" tall × 3½" deep (16.5cm × 20.5cm × 9cm)

Larger: 9½" wide × 9½" tall × 5½" deep (24cm × 24cm × 14cm)

Level of Difficulty (experienced)

Fabric Choices

This purse is perfect for quilting cotton fabric. If you choose home décor weight fabric, omit the woven fusible interfacing for the exterior body and bottom pieces. Hint: The lining becomes an accent fabric because it is seen from the outside at the top even when it is closed, so be creative when you choose your lining fabric.

Skills to Review

Cutting Bias Binding (page 15)
Installing Eyelets/Grommets (page 18)
Sewing and Clipping Curves (page 14)
Topstitching (page 14)
Working with Peltex (page 15)

Materials

Yardage

⅔ yard (61cm) fabric for exterior

1 yard (91.5cm) fabric for ruffle

½ yard (45.5cm) fabric for lining

1 yard (91.5cm) woven fusible interfacing, 20" (51cm) wide

⅓ yard (30.5cm) fusible fleece

10½" × 7" (26.5 × 18cm) piece of Peltex

Hardware

8 eyelet sets, ⁷⁄₁₆" (1.1cm)

5 eyelet sets, ¼" (6mm), optional for adjustable strap

1 metal center post buckle, 1" (2.5cm), optional for adjustable strap

2 metal rectangles, 1" (2.5cm), optional for adjustable strap

Notions

¾ yard (68.5cm) piping cord, ³⁄₃₂" (2.4mm)

1 cord stop, optional

Patterns

Free-Spirit Drawstring Purse patterns: Bottom Smallish, Bottom Bigger (on CD)

Featured fabric by Chelsea Andersen of Pink Fig Design

Cutting

Note: Measurements are given as width × length. See cutting charts on the CD, if desired.

From exterior fabric, cut:
Small Bag
1 rectangle 17½" × 9" (44.5cm × 23cm) for Body Exterior
2 Rectangle A 34" × 6" (86.5cm × 15cm) for Ruffles
1 Rectangle B 34" × 7" (86.5cm × 18cm) for Ruffles
1 rectangle 1¼" × 19" (3.2cm × 48.5cm) for Piping
    Note: This can be cut on bias.

Larger Bag
1 rectangle 26" × 10½" (66cm × 26.5cm) for Body Exterior
2 Rectangle A 50" × 6" (127cm × 15cm) for Ruffles
1 Rectangle B 50" × 7" (127cm × 18cm) for Ruffles
1 rectangle 1¼" × 27" (3.2cm × 68.5cm) for Piping.
    Note: This can be cut on bias.

All Bags
1 rectangle 2¾" × 70" (7cm × 178cm) for Shoulder Strap. Note: This can be pieced.
1 rectangle 1" × 40" (2.5cm × 101.5cm) for Drawstring
1 Bottom from pattern

From lining fabric, cut:
Small Bag: 1 rectangle 17" × 8" (43cm × 20.5cm) for Body
Larger Bag: 1 rectangle 25" × 9½" (63.5cm × 24cm) for Body
1 Bottom from pattern
1 rectangle 7½" × 5½" (19cm × 14cm) for Pocket

From woven fusible interfacing, cut:
Small Bag: 1 rectangle 17½" × 9" (44.5cm × 23cm) for Body
Larger Bag: 1 rectangle 26" × 10½" (66cmx 26.5cm) for Body
1 Bottom from pattern

From fusible fleece, cut:
Small Bag: 1 rectangle 17½" × 9" (44.5cm × 23cm) for Body
Larger Bag: 1 rectangle 26" × 10½" (66cm × 26.5cm) for Body

1 rectangle 1" × 70" (2.5cm × 178cm) for Shoulder Strap. Note: This can be pieced.

From Peltex, cut:
1 Bottom from pattern

Note

The illustrations show the smallish purse.

Preparing the Pieces

1 Fuse the woven fusible interfacing to the Body and Bottom Exterior pieces according to the manufacturer's instructions.

2 Fuse the fusible fleece to the Body Exterior piece according to the manufacturer's instructions.

3 Trim ⅝" (1.5cm) off the perimeter of the Bottom Peltex piece.

4 Topstitch the Peltex piece to the center wrong side of the Bottom Exterior piece at ⅛" (3mm).

5 Trim ¼" (6mm) off the perimeter of the Bottom Lining.

6 Do not fuse the fusible fleece to the Shoulder Strap yet.

Body

7 If sewing the Ruffle Exterior: On the right side of Body Exterior, draw a line 6" (15cm) above the bottom raw edge. Draw another line 7" (7¾" for larger size) (18cm [19.5cm]) above the bottom raw edge. (Fig. 1)

8 Fold the BODY EXTERIOR piece in half, bringing the short sides together, right sides facing. Sew with a ½" (1.3cm) seam allowance. Press the seam open.

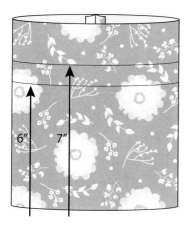

Figure 1

Ruffles (Optional)

9 Serge or zigzag the short ends of each RUFFLE to prevent fraying (do the same to any other ends if the Ruffle was pieced). Bring the short ends of each Ruffle together, right sides facing. Sew with a ½" (1.3cm) seam allowance. Press the seam open.

Tip: If the Ruffle strips were pieced, make sure the seams are not in front.

10 Fold the lower edge of one Ruffle over, wrong sides facing, ¼" (6mm) and press. Fold again ¼" (6mm) and press. Topstitch at ⅛" (3mm). Repeat for all three Ruffles. (Fig. 2)

11 Beginning at the seam from step 9, sew two rows of gathering stitches along the top edge of each Ruffle; sew the first row ⅜" (1cm) from the top edge, and sew the second row ¾" (2cm) from the top edge. (Fig. 2)

12 Align one Ruffle A raw edge, wrong side, onto the right side of the Body piece following the 6" (15cm) line made in step 8. Match the seams of both pieces. Evenly gather the Ruffle around the perimeter. From the right side, topstitch the Ruffle to the Body at ½" (1.3cm). (Fig. 3) Zigzag the raw edge of the Ruffle to the Body. Remove the gathering stitches.

13 Repeat with the remaining Ruffle A, placing it 1" (1¾" for bigger size) (2.5cm [4.5cm]) above the previous Ruffle following the second line drawn.

Figure 3

14 Evenly gather Ruffle B and place the wrong side along the top edge of the Body right side, matching the seams. Baste in place with a ¼" (6mm) seam allowance.

Tip: Wait to remove the gathering stitches until after the Lining has been sewn in place.

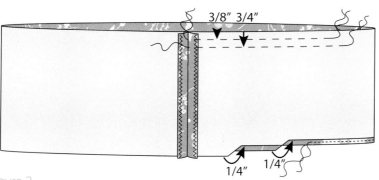

Figure 2

Shoulder Strap

15 Trim off the lower corner of fusible fleece at a 45-degree angle.

16 Lay the SHOULDER STRAP horizontally, right-side down. According to the manufacturer's instructions, fuse the fusible fleece to the wrong side as shown. Fold and press the Shoulder Strap as shown. The finished width should be 1" (2.5cm). Topstitch down the center. The top, bottom and left raw edges should be folded inside and hidden. (Fig. 4)

Tip: If omitting the metal rectangles, follow the above directions with the exception of anything related to the 45-degree angle. Determine the desired length of the strap plus 1" (2.5cm). Trim off the excess, and skip to step 18.

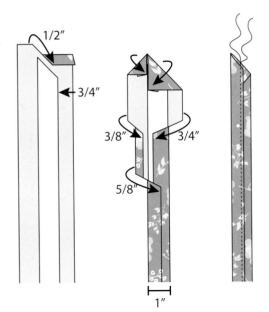

Figure 4

Shoulder Strap Tabs

Figure 5

17 Trim two 3½" (9cm) lengths off the square end of the Shoulder Strap for the Tabs Thread a TAB through each metal rectangle and fold it in half, seam against the seam. (Fig. 5)

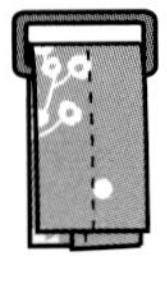

18 Align each Tab (or Shoulder Strap end) 1¼" (1½" for larger size) (3.2cm [3.8cm]) away from the center back of the Exterior Body piece, right sides facing, matching the raw edges of the Tabs with the raw edges of the Body piece. Baste in place at a ¼" (6mm) seam allowance. (Fig. 6)

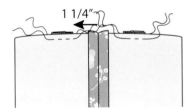

Figure 6

Piping

19 Fold the PIPING piece around the cord, wrong sides facing. With a piping or zipper foot, sew next to the cording at about ½" (1.3cm), keeping the cord snug next to the foot. Clip the seam allowance every ½" (1.3cm) all the way along the piping. (Fig. 7)

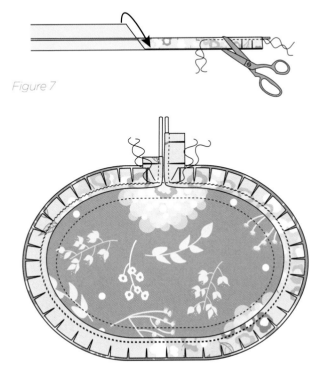

Figure 7

Figure 8

20 Beginning at the center, align the raw edges of the Piping and the BOTTOM Exterior piece, right sides facing, as illustrated. (Fig. 8)

Using the stitching on the Piping as a guide and with the piping/zipper foot, sew the Piping onto the Bottom. It should be about a ½" (1.3cm) seam allowance. (Fig. 8) Trim off the extra Piping.

21 Make ⅜" (1cm) clips every ½" (1.3cm) along the lower edge of the Body piece. Align the Body seam with the center back of the Bottom, right sides facing. Align the center front of both pieces. Using the clips in the fabric to ease, pin the perimeter. Following the stitching from step 20, sew the perimeter, attaching the Body to the Bottom with Piping in between. (Fig. 9) Turn right-side out.

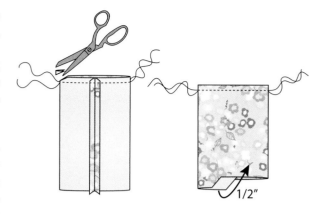

Figure 10   Figure 11

23 Position the seam side of the lower edge of the Pocket 1" (1¼" for bigger size) (2.5cm [3.2cm]) up from the bottom raw edge of the right side of the BODY LINING piece and 2⅝" (4¾" for bigger size) (6.7cm [12cm]) in from the right side raw edge. Topstitch the sides and bottom of the Pocket at ⅛" (3mm).

24 Bring the Body Lining piece short sides together, right sides facing. Sew the top 2" (5cm) and bottom 2" (5cm) with a ½" (1.3cm) seam allowance. This leaves an opening for turning. (Fig. 12) Press the seam open.

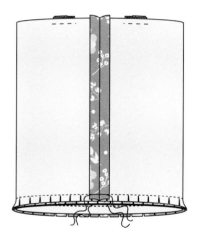

Figure 9

Lining

22 Bring the short ends of the POCKET together, right sides facing. Sew with a ¼" (6mm) seam allowance. Press the seam open. Maneuver the seam around to the center. Sew the top raw edge with a ½" (1.3cm) seam allowance. This will be the top of the pocket. Clip the corners. (Fig. 10) Turn right-side out. Topstitch the top edge at ¼" (6mm). Tuck the raw edge under ½" (1.3cm), wrong sides facing. (Fig. 11) Pin the opening closed.

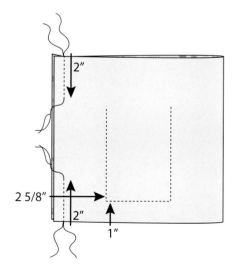

Figure 12

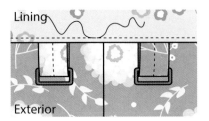

Lining

Exterior

Figure 14

25 Make ⅜" (1cm) clips every ½" (1.3cm) along the lower edge of the Body Lining. Align the Body Lining seam with the side of the BOTTOM LINING piece, right sides facing. Using the clips in the fabric to ease, pin the perimeter. Sew with a ½" (1.3cm) seam allowance. (Fig. 13)

If Ruffles were sewn, topstitch through the Exterior and Lining layers from the right side, pulling only the Tabs and Ruffle out of the way. Remove the gathering stitches from Ruffle B. (Fig. 15)

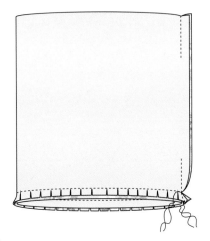

Figure 13

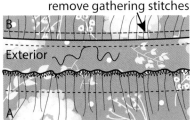

remove gathering stitches

B

Exterior

A

Figure 15

Assembling the Body

26 Tuck the Exterior inside the Lining, right sides facing. The center of the pocket in the Lining will match up with the center back of the Body Exterior. Align the top raw edges of both pieces. Ease a little to fit well. Tuck the Tabs inside. Sew the top perimeter with a ½" (1.3cm) seam allowance.

27 Pull right-side out through the Lining opening. Topstitch the seam allowance and Tab raw edges to the Lining. (Fig. 14)

> Tip: This is a little tricky because the machine position will be accessed through the Lining opening, which is relatively small. Reposition the Body Exterior every couple of inches (centimeters) out of the way so it doesn't get caught in the topstitching. Do not topstitch through the Exterior layer.

28 Topstitch the Lining closed and tuck inside. Tack down the Lining to the Exterior 1½" (3.8cm) from the top at the center back.

Shoulder Strap Buckle Strip

If omitting hardware skip to step 34.

29 Trim one 13" (33cm) length off the square end of the Shoulder Strap. Sew a ¼" (6mm) buttonhole centered 1¾" (4.5cm) down from one end. Thread the strip through the buckle. Slide the catch of the buckle through the buttonhole and fold over the post 1¾" (4.5cm), seam against seam. Fold that raw edge over ¼" (6mm), seam against seam. Hide all raw edges. Topstitch at ⅛" (3mm). When the buckle faces outward, the catch will be in the up position.

30 Thread the other end of this buckle strip through one of the rectangles on a Tab. Fold over 1" (2.5cm), seam against seam. The buckle faces outward and the folds are inward when worn. Fold that raw edge over ½" (1.3cm), seam against seam. Hide all raw edges. Topstitch at ⅛" (3mm). (Fig. 16)

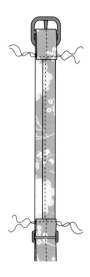

Figure 16

Shoulder Strap Completion

31 Experiment with the length of the Shoulder Strap and trim if it is too long. Thread the square end of the Shoulder Strap through the remaining metal rectangle. Fold over 1" (2.5cm), seam against seam. The folds are inward as it is worn. Fold that raw edge over ½" (1.3cm), seam against seam. Hide all raw edges. Topstitch at ⅛" (3mm).

32 Thread the angled tip of the Strap through the buckle. Determine the desired length. Install ¼" (6mm) eyelets (see page 18) at that location and several more about 1¼" (3.2cm) apart.

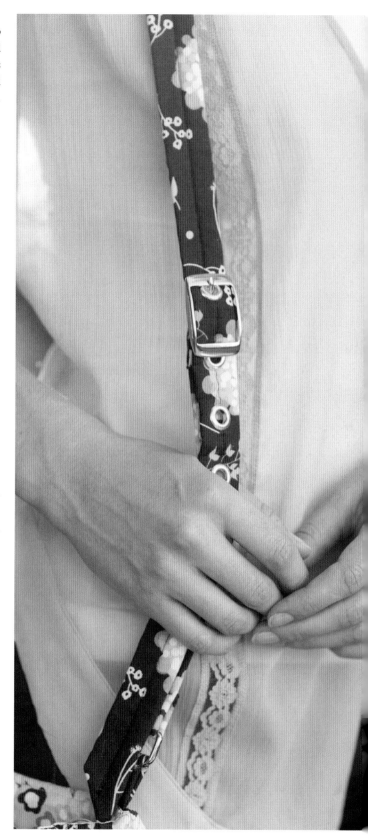

Large Eyelets

33 For the smaller bag, install the large ⁷⁄₁₆" (1.1cm) eyelets (see page 18) 1" (2.5cm) down from the top edge of the bag through all layers for the smallish bag at intervals as shown. (Fig. 17)

For the larger bag, install the large ⁷⁄₁₆" (1.1cm) eyelets 1½" (3.8cm) down from the top edge of the bag through all layers at intervals as shown. (Fig. 18)

Tip: For eyelets with Exterior Ruffles, catch the folds of the Ruffles under the eyelet edges. Cut the hole for the eyelets through all layers, including the Ruffle layers, with the Ruffles following the natural flow of the gathering. To maintain that position, whip stitch by hand all of the layers around the hole opening where it will be hidden under the eyelet edge. This might feel a little tedious, but it is important. Otherwise, when a little pressure is put on the ruffle, the raw edges created by cutting the eyelet hole will pull through. The eyelet can only hold on so tight.

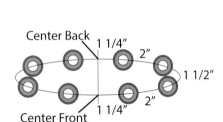

Figure 17

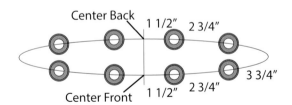

Figure 18

Drawstring

34 Fold the DRAWSTRING long edges over ¼" (6mm), wrong sides facing, and press. Fold in half and press. Topstitch down the center. (Fig. 19)

35 Beginning from the exterior side of the bag, thread the Drawstring through the eyelet just right of center toward the Lining. Then thread it out toward the exterior through the next eyelet to the right. Continue threading in and out until exiting the eyelet left of center.

Tip: If desired, thread both ends through a drawstring toggle.

36 Adjust to the desired length, keeping in mind the extra needed when the bag is open. Trim the excess. Cut each end at an angle. Tie a knot 1" (2.5cm) from the end to keep it from fraying too much.

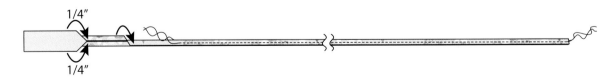

Figure 19

Piccadilly Purse

The *Piccadilly Purse* manages to be both regal and bohemian as it easily transitions from casual to dressy. The ruffled body and handles create a feminine flair. Its roomy interior is hidden by the flattering shape. The zipper closure provides security and privacy, the shoulder strap is removable and the piping creates a polished accent. Hang a couple of charms on the outside, and you will make a personal statement with this accessory.

Size

14" wide × 10" tall × 7" deep
(35.5cm × 25.5cm × 18cm)

Level of Difficulty (intermediate)

Fabric Choices

This pattern is designed for quilting cotton fabric. If you choose a home décor or heavier fabric, leave off the fusible interfacing. Cotton is easiest for the lining.

Skills to Review

Installing Purse Feet *(page 18)*
Sewing and Clipping Curves *(page 14)*
Topstitching *(page 14)*
Turning Narrow Pieces Right-Side Out *(page 15)*

Materials

Yardage

1½ yards (1.4m) fabric for exterior

1¼ yards (1.1m) fabric for lining

1½ yards (1.4m) woven fusible interfacing, 20" (51cm) wide

1" × 37" (2.5cm × 94cm) piece of fusible fleece

18" × 7" (45.5cm × 18cm) piece of Peltex

27" × 30" (68.5cm × 76cm) piece of Soft and Stable

Hardware

6 O-rings, 1¼" (3.2cm)

2 swivel hooks, 1" (2.5cm)

4 purse feet, 18mm, optional

2 swivel hooks, ½" (1.3cm), optional

Notions

1 sport zipper, 14" (35.5cm)

1 zipper, 7" (18cm)

40" (101.5cm) of piping cord, $^{22}/_{32}$" (1.7cm), for handles

2 yards piping cord, $^{5}/_{32}$" (4mm), for sides

2 yards (1.8m) extra-wide, double-fold, ½" (1.3cm) bias tape

Patterns

Piccadilly Purse patterns: Side, Handle Tab, Ruffle Overlay, Ruffle Support, Top Template (on CD)

Featured fabric exterior by Chelsea Andersen of Pink Fig Design; lining by Amanda Herring of The Quilted Fish

Cutting

> Note: Measurements are given as width × length. See cutting charts on the CD, if desired.

From exterior fabric, cut:

2 Ruffle Overlay pieces from pattern on fold for Exterior Lower Body

2 Ruffle Support pieces from pattern for Exterior Lower Body

2 Rectangle A 15½" × 7½" (39.5cm × 19cm) for Exterior Upper Body

1 Rectangle B 15½" × 6½" (39.5cm × 16.5cm) for Exterior Bottom

2 Side pieces from pattern

1 rectangle 2½" × 5" (6.5cm × 12.5cm) for Zipper Pull Tabs

6 rectangles 2¾" × 4½" (7cm × 11.5cm) for Handle Tabs

2 rectangles 3" × 45" (7.5cm × 114.5cm) for Handles. Note: These can be pieced.

1 rectangle 3" × 38" (7.5cm × 96.5cm) for Shoulder Strap. Note: This can be pieced.

1 rectangle 2" × 16" (5cm × 40.5cm) for Charm Hanger, optional

From lining fabric, cut:

1 rectangle 15½" × 29½" (39.5cm × 75cm) for Body Lining

2 Side pieces from pattern

2 rectangles 1½" × 33" (3.8cm × 84cm) for Piping. Note: These can be cut on bias.

2 rectangles 9¼" × 12" (23.5cm × 30.5cm) for Interior Pockets

From woven fusible fleece, cut:

2 Ruffle Overlay pieces from pattern on fold for Exterior Lower Body

2 rectangles 15½" × 7½" (39.5cm × 19cm) for Exterior Upper Body

1 rectangle 15½" × 6½" (39.5cm × 16.5cm) for Exterior Bottom

2 Side pieces for Exterior from pattern

From fusible fleece, cut:

1 rectangle 1" × 37" (2.5cm × 94cm) for Shoulder Strap

From Peltex, cut:

1 rectangle 14¼" × 5¼" (36cm × 13.5cm) for Bottom

6 Handle Tabs from pattern

From woven Soft and Stable, cut:

2 Ruffle Support pieces from pattern for Exterior Lower Body

2 rectangles 15½" × 7½" (39.5cm × 19cm) for Exterior Upper Body

1 rectangle 15½" × 6½" (39.5cm × 16.5cm) for Exterior Bottom

2 Side pieces from pattern

> ### Tip
>
> *If you're thinking about substituting Soft and Stable with fusible fleece for the body, remember that Soft and Stable will give more stability to the purse. However, the tricky steps of putting the sides on the body are bulky and awkward, and they are a little more difficult when using Soft and Stable. Fusible fleece is less firm, so it is easier to work with, but it will not hold the sides of the purse up independently.*

Preparing the Pieces

1 According to the manufacturer's instructions, fuse the woven fusible interfacing to the wrong side of the Ruffle Overlay pieces, Rectangles A and B, and the Side Exterior pieces.

2 Pin the Soft and Stable to the wrong side of the Side Exterior pieces, Exterior Upper Body rectangles, Exterior Bottom rectangle and Ruffle Support pieces. Pull the fabric a little snug across the Soft and Stable. (If substituting with fusible fleece, fuse to the wrong side of the pieces.)

Handle Tabs

3 Position one Peltex Handle Tabs piece with the curved end down ½" (1.3cm) from the top edge of a HANDLE TAB piece on the wrong side. Stretch and pin the outer edges of fabric around to the back side of the Peltex along the rounded sides. Pull tight for a smooth curve. Fold the long edges of the Tab over ¾" (2cm), wrong sides facing, and press. The finished width should be 1¼" (3.2cm). There will be fullness along the curve on the back side. (Fig. 1) Cut away some of the fullness but not too close to the outer edge.

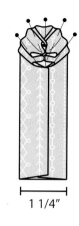

1 1/4"

Figure 1

4 Thread the Tab through an O-ring. Fold the Tab's raw edge down, wrong sides facing, so the finished length is 2¼" (5.5cm) and pin. All the raw edges should be hidden.

Tip: Fold the corners in slightly to hide the raw edges.

5 Repeat steps 3–4 for all six Tabs.

6 Position two Handle Tabs as illustrated along the long edge of one RECTANGLE A (Upper Exterior Body rectangle), placing the Tab ¾" (2cm) from the top edge and 3¼" (8.5cm) from the side. Topstitch at ⅛" (3mm) as shown. (Fig. 2)

Tip: Use a slightly shorter stitch length for a smoother line around the curve. Sew across the straight edge twice for added reinforcement.

All raw edges will be concealed. Repeat for two more Tabs and the remaining Rectangle A.

7 Set aside the remaining two Tabs until step 23.

Top Piece

8 Center the sport zipper along the top of one Rectangle A, right sides facing. Sew with a ¼" (6mm) seam allowance. (Fig. 3) Center the other half of the sport zipper along the top of the remaining Rectangle A, right sides facing. Sew with a ¼" (6mm) seam allowance. Press the piece flat.

9 Place the Top Template over the piece, matching the center of the Template with the zipper. Draw the arches on both ends. Trim off the extra pieces. (Fig. 4)

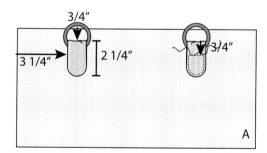

Figure 2

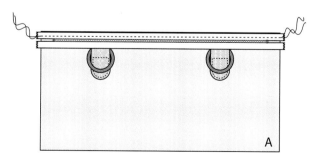

Figure 3

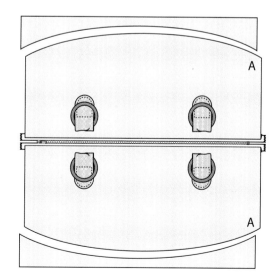

Figure 4

Ruffle Panels

10 Cut ⅜" (1cm) clips every ¼" (6mm) along the arched edge of the RUFFLE SUPPORT piece. Sew a pair of gathering stitches along the top and bottom of the RUFFLE OVERLAY. Pull the threads to evenly gather the Overlay. Place the Overlay wrong side over the Ruffle Support right side, aligning the top and bottom edges, and pin. Baste the top edge with a ½" (1.3cm) seam allowance. Remove the gathering stitches. (Fig. 5)

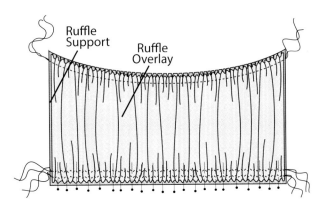

Figure 5

11 Use the clips in the fabric to evenly align the arched edge of the Ruffle piece with the arched edge of the Top piece. Sew with a ½" (1.3cm) seam allowance twice.

Tip: Offset the pieces by ½" (1.3cm) at the beginning of the seam so the edges will line up perfectly when opened. (Fig. 6) This is similar to seams sewn when piecing bias binding (see page 15).

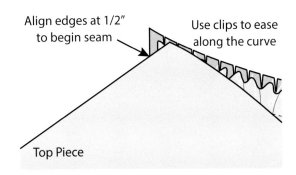

Figure 6

Tip: The curved edge of the Ruffle piece stretches in the opposite direction when attaching to the Top piece; therefore, the pieces do not lay flat during sewing. The basting on the Ruffle piece helps keep the integrity of the gathers during this process.

Trim the Soft and Stable in the seam allowance to ⅛" (3mm). Remove the gathering stitches. Leave the bottom Ruffle edge pinned in place.

12 Repeat for the remaining Ruffle Overlay, Ruffle Support and the other arched edge of the Top piece. (Fig. 7)

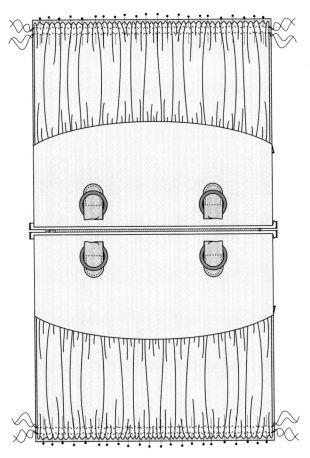

Figure 7

58

Bottom

13 Center the Peltex Bottom to the wrong side of RECTANGLE B (Bottom). Topstitch the perimeter of the Peltex at ⅛" (3mm). (Fig. 8)

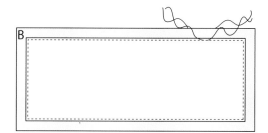

Figure 8

14 Align one long side of Rectangle B with the bottom end of one Ruffle panel, right sides facing. Sew with a ½" (1.3cm) seam allowance. Trim the Soft and Stable of both Rectangle B and the Ruffle panel in the seam allowance to ⅛" (3mm). Remove the gathering stitches from the Ruffle panel.

15 Repeat for the remaining long side of Rectangle B and the bottom of the other Ruffle panel.

16 From the right side of the Bottom, attach the four purse feet (see page 18) through the Peltex, placing each ¾" (2cm) from the long edge and 3" (7.5cm) from the short edge. (Fig. 9)

Tip: The purse feet will not completely protect the bottom of your purse, so be careful where you set it down.

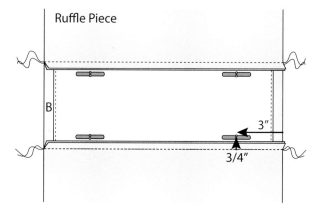

Figure 9

Lining Zipper Pocket

17 Align one INTERIOR POCKET with the BODY LINING piece, right sides facing and short sides up as shown. Draw a rectangle 7¼" × ½" (18.5cm × 1.3cm) on the wrong side of the Pocket as illustrated. (Fig. 10) Topstitch this drawn rectangle. Cut down the center of the sewn rectangle and into each corner, being careful not to clip through stitching. (Fig. 10) Insert the Pocket piece through the slit to the wrong side of the Lining and press around opening, creating a finished window slot.

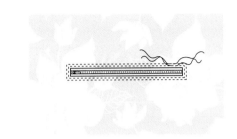

Figure 11

19 Fold the Pocket fabric in half, right sides facing. Moving the Lining out of the way, sew the three raw edges of the Pocket with a ½" (1.3cm) seam allowance. (Fig. 12)

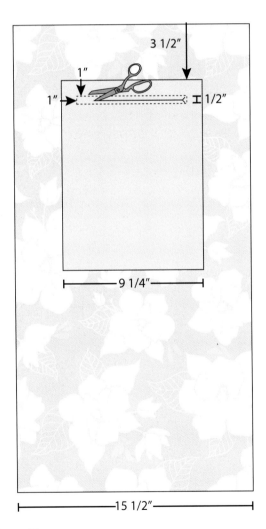

Figure 10

18 Center the 7" (18cm) zipper in this opening. From the right side of the Lining, topstitch at ⅛" (3mm) and ¼" (6mm). (Fig. 11)

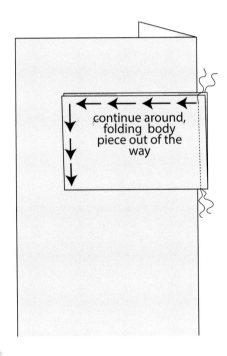

Figure 12

Lining Small Pocket

20 Bring the short sides of the remaining Interior Pocket together, right sides facing. Sew the two sides and the bottom with a ¼" (6mm) seam allowance leaving a 4" (10cm) opening for turning. (Fig. 13) Turn right-side out. Press flat. If dividing this pocket into sections, fold the Pocket in division

locations and press so there will be a creased line as a sewing guide. Topstitch the folded edge at ¼"(6mm). Pin the opening closed. (Fig. 14)

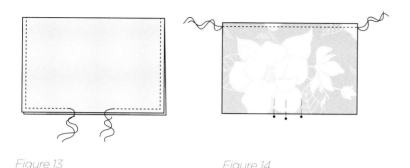

Figure 13   Figure 14

21 Place the top of the Pocket centered 5" (12.5cm) down from the remaining short edge of the right side of the Lining Body. From the right side, topstitch the two sides, the bottom and on each side of the crease line at ⅛" (3mm). This will close the opening at the bottom of the Pocket and create pocket divisions. (Fig. 15)

Tip: Both short sides of the lining piece are the "top" because the piece loops around. So, position the opening edge of the pocket accordingly.

Sides

22 Pin the SIDE EXTERIOR and SIDE LINING pieces, wrong sides facing, with Soft and Stable between them.

23 Center the folded edge of one Handle Tab down 1¾" (4.5cm) from the top edge of the Side Exterior. Topstitch at ⅛" (3mm) as shown. (Fig. 16)

Tip: Use a slightly shorter stitch length for a smoother line around the curve. Sew across the straight part twice for added reinforcement. All raw edges should be concealed.

24 Repeat for the other Side Exterior and remaining Handle Tab.

5"

Figure 15

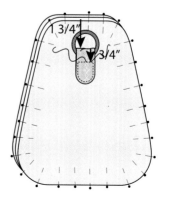

1 3/4"
3/4"

Figure 16

Piping

25 Fold one PIPING piece around the narrow cord, wrong sides facing. With the piping/zipper foot, sew next to the cording with about a ½" (1.3cm) seam allowance, keeping the cord snug next to the foot. Clip the seam allowance every ½" (1.3cm) along the Piping. (Fig. 17)

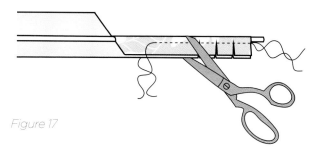

Figure 17

26 Beginning at the center bottom, align the Piping with the Side Exterior piece right side as illustrated. (Fig. 18)

27 Using the stitching on the Piping as a guide and with the piping/zipper foot, sew the Piping onto the Side piece. It should be about a ½" (1.3cm) seam allowance. (Fig. 18) Trim off the extra piping.

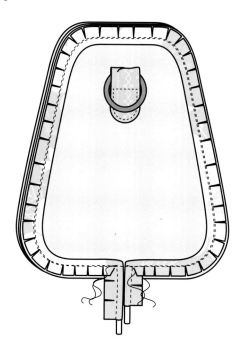

Figure 18

28 Repeat with the remaining narrow piping cord, Piping rectangle and Side Exterior.

Zipper Pull Tabs

29 Fold the ZIPPER PULL TAB in half, right sides facing, and sew the long raw edge with a ¼" (6mm) seam allowance. (Fig. 19) Turn right-side out.

Tip: This is a perfect place to use the safety pin technique on page 14.

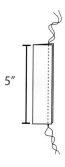

5"

Figure 19

30 Move the seam around so it is centered. Press flat. Cut the piece in half so there are two Zipper Tabs. Fold both pieces in half, seam to seam, and press again.

31 Center one folded Zipper Tab at the top of each Side Exterior right sides matching raw edges. Sew with a ¼" (6mm) seam allowance several times for added reinforcement. (Fig. 20)

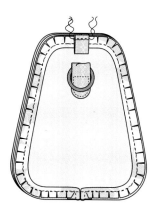

Figure 20

Assembling the Body

32 Align the top edge of the Body Exterior (Fig. 21) with one short end of the Body Lining, right sides facing. The sport zipper should be between the two pieces. Sew with a ¼" (6mm) seam allowance. (Fig. 22) Trim the Soft and Stable in the seam allowance to ⅛" (3mm).

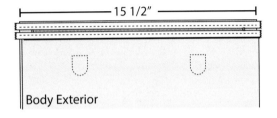

Figure 21

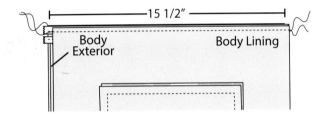

Figure 22

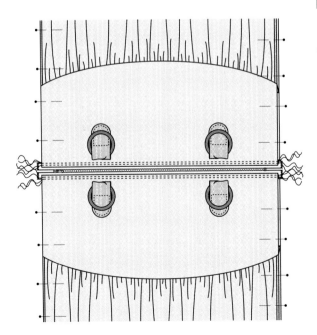

Figure 23

33 Repeat with the other short end of the Body Lining and Exterior piece.

34 Turn right-side out. Topstitch through all the layers at ⅛" (3mm) and ¼" (6mm) along both sides of the sport zipper.

35 Pin the Body Exterior and Lining layers together along the sides. (Fig. 23)

> Tip: It is necessary to ease a little because the Lining is slightly smaller than the Exterior. Cut tiny clips in the seam allowance, if needed, to help with the easing.

36 Turn wrong-side out. Align the Body to one Side, exterior sides facing. Begin by aligning the center bottoms and tops. Cut ⅜" (1cm) clips every ½" (1.3cm) along the raw edge of the Body in areas that will be aligned with the curves of the Side for easing. Using the stitching from step 28 as a guide, sew with a ½" (1.3cm) seam allowance. (Fig. 24) Trim the seam allowance to ¼" (6mm). Trim the Soft and Stable in the seam allowance to ⅛" (3mm).

> Tip: Through this and the binding steps, double-check often that the piping is not being covered up with stitching. If noticed between steps, mistakes can easily be fixed.

37 Repeat for the other Side.

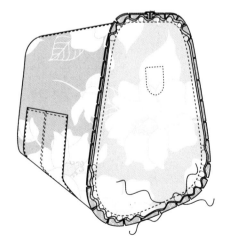

Figure 24

Binding (Seam Finish)

38 Open the bias tape. Fold one end, wrong sides facing, ½" (1.3cm) and press. This will be a clean start of the seam finish. Begin at the bottom of the bag. Align the first manufactured fold of the bias tape with the Body seam stitching on the Lining side. Pin the perimeter. Use the stretch of the bias to ease evenly. Overlap the bias tape ½" (1.3cm) at the end. Sew along this fold.

39 Fold the bias tape around the seam allowance so it overlaps the previous stitching by about ⅛" (3mm) and stitch in the ditch. (Fig. 25)

40 Repeat for the other Side. Turn right-side out.

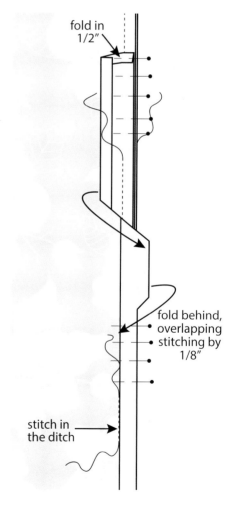

fold in
1/2"

fold behind,
overlapping
stitching by
1/8"

stitch in
the ditch

Figure 25

Handles

41 Fold both ends of the HANDLE piece, wrong sides facing, ¼" (6mm) and press. Fold the Handle in half lengthwise, right sides facing. Sew the long edge with a ¼" (6mm) seam allowance. (Fig. 26) Attach a safety pin to one end near the seam. Thread the safety pin into the center of the sewn tube and guide it through to turn the piece right-side out.

42 Cut the wide cording in half. Sew one end of one piece at ¼" (6mm) several times for reinforcement. Attach the safety pin to the cording just past the stitching and guide the cording through the Handle. (Fig. 27) Gather the extra fullness of the fabric in the center area. Pull the cording so the fabric extends 1" (2.5cm) beyond the cording on the starting end. Securely pin so the cording doesn't move. Finish the other end so the fabric extends 1" (2.5cm) beyond the cording. Remove the safety pin used to guide the cording. Pin this end of the cording in place as well.

> Tip: To give added strength to the cording, I highly recommend sewing a 20" (51cm) piece of ½" (1.3cm) seam tape to the ends of the cording prior to threading it into the fabric.

43 Flatten the ends of the Handle tube so the seam is centered. Thread one end of the Handle through one Body O-ring and fold 1" (2.5cm) back on itself, seam against seam. Flatten the end of the cord. Tuck the corners under to help hide the folded edge. Topstitch a rectangle to secure. (Fig. 28) Repeat for other end of the Handle.

44 Repeat for the other Handle and length of wide cording.

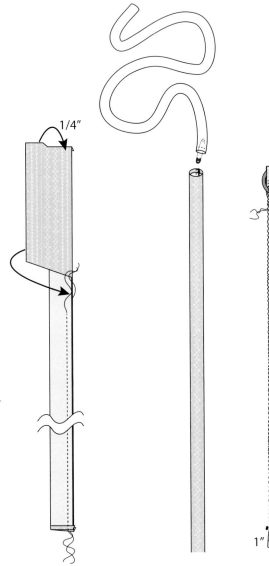

Figure 26   Figure 27   Figure 28

Shoulder Strap

45 Fuse fusible fleece to the wrong side of the SHOULDER STRAP, placing it ½" (1.3cm) from one long edge and both short edges. Fold with wrong sides facing and press as illustrated. The finished width should be 1" (2.5cm). Topstitch both long sides at ⅛" (3mm), hiding all raw edges. (Fig. 29)

46 Thread one end through a 1" (2.5cm) swivel hook, overlapping 1¼" (3.2cm). Topstitch at ⅛" (3mm). (Fig. 30) Repeat for the other swivel hook. Clip the swivel hooks onto the O-rings on the sides of the bag.

Charm Hanger, Optional

47 Fold the CHARM HANGER wrong sides facing and press as illustrated. The finished width should be ½" (1.3cm). Topstitch both long sides at ⅛" (3mm), hiding all raw edges. (Fig. 31)

48 Thread the Hanger through a ½" swivel hook, overlapping ½" (1.3cm). Machine whipstitch in place, hiding all raw edges. (Fig. 32) Repeat for the other swivel hook on the other end of the Hanger. Loop it through an O-ring and you're done. (Fig. 33)

Figure 29

Figure 30

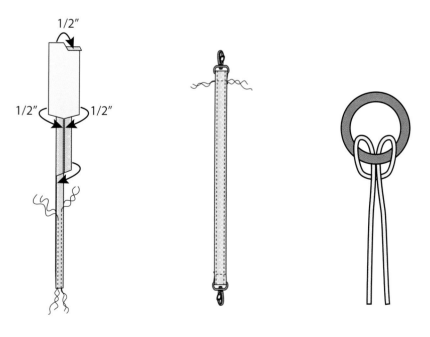

Figure 31   Figure 32   Figure 33

Boutique Day Purse

For the creative sewer who cannot stop her enthusiasm for fabrics and color, my *Boutique Day Purse* is the perfect project. Find a fantastic fabric for the purse, and then go wild making different changeable covers for every outfit and mood. Its versatility is a plus, but its size, shape and features are what will have you falling hard for this purse. The covers are attached by invisible magnets. The zipper strip at the top conceals everything inside, and the elastic sides give the purse its fun shape.

Size

10½" wide × 7½" tall × 5" deep (26.5cm × 19cm × 12.5cm)

Level of Difficulty (experienced)

Fabric Choices

The body of the bag is best made from cotton or home décor fabric. If home décor fabric is chosen, eliminate the fusible interfacing on those pieces.

For the changeable cover, almost anything will work. If laminate or home décor fabric is chosen, eliminate the fusible interfacing on those pieces. However, if heavier fabric or laminate is the choice for the changeable cover, line it with cotton for better magnetic attraction.

Skills to Review

Installing a Magnetic Snap Set, sew-in application (page 18)
Installing Purse Feet (page 18)
Sewing and Clipping Curves (page 14)
Topstitching (page 14)
Turning Narrow Pieces Right-Side Out (page 15)
Working with Peltex (page 15)

Materials

Yardage

½ yard (45.5cm) fabric for exterior

½ yard (45.5cm) fabric for lining

1¼ yards (1.1m) woven fusible interfacing

21" × 12" (53.5cm × 30.5cm) piece of Peltex

Hardware

4 O-rings, 1¼" (3.2cm)

2 sets of sew-in magnets

Notions

1 zipper, 12" (30.5cm)

24" (61cm) piping cord, $^{22}/_{32}$" (1.7cm)

10" (25.5cm) elastic, ¼" (6mm) wide

For each cover

½ yard (45.5cm) fabric

½ yard (45.5cm) woven fusible interfacing

21" × 12" (53.5cm × 30.5cm) piece of Peltex

4 purse feet, 14mm

2 sets of sew-in magnets

1 center post buckle, 1" (2.5cm) optional

1 eyelet set, ¼" (6mm), optional if including buckle

Patterns

Boutique Day Purse patterns: Body, Side Exterior, Side Lining (on CD)

Featured fabric by Amanda Herring of The Quilted Fish

Cutting

> Note: Measurements are given as width × length. See cutting charts on the CD, if desired.

From the main fabric, cut:

1 Body from pattern, on fold
2 Side pieces from pattern
4 rectangles 10½" × 3" (26.5cm × 7.5cm) for Zipper Strip
1 rectangle 1½" × 3½" (3.8cm × 9cm) for Zipper End
2 Body Lining Top pieces from pattern
2 rectangles 11½" × 7½" (29cm × 19cm) for Body Lining Bottom
2 Side Lining pieces from pattern
2 rectangles 2¾" × 18" (7cm × 45.5cm) for Handles
1 rectangle 3¼" × 16" (8.5cm × 40.5cm) for Handle Tabs
1 rectangle 13" × 4" (33cm × 10cm) for Pocket

From accent fabric, cut:

1 Changeable Cover Outside from pattern, on fold
2 Changeable Cover Inside Front/Back pieces from pattern
1 rectangle 11½" × 5½" (29cm × 14cm) for Changeable Cover Inside Bottom
1 rectangle 2½" × 19½" (6.5cm × 49.5cm) for Changeable Cover Buckle Strap Bottom, optional
1 rectangle 2½" × 7½" (6.5cm × 19cm) for Changeable Cover Buckle Strap Top, optional

From woven fusible interfacing, cut:

1 Body from pattern, on fold
2 Side pieces from pattern
2 rectangles 10½" × 3" (26.5cm × 7.5cm) for Zipper Strip
2 Body Lining Top pieces from pattern
2 rectangles 11½" × 7½" (29cm × 19cm) for Body Lining Bottom
2 rectangles 2¾" × 18" (7cm × 45.5cm) for Handles
1 Changeable Cover Outside from pattern, on fold
1 rectangle 2½" × 19½" (6.5cm × 49.5cm) for Changeable Cover Buckle Strap Bottom, optional
1 rectangle 2½" × 7½" (6.5cm × 19cm) for Changeable Cover Buckle Strap Top, optional

From Peltex, cut:

2 Body Support pieces from pattern
1 rectangle 10" × 4¼" (25.5cm × 11cm) for Support Bottom
2 Changeable Cover Front/Back pieces from pattern
1 rectangle 10½ " × 4¼" (26.5cm × 11cm) for Changeable Cover Bottom

Preparing the Pieces

1 Fuse woven fusible interfacing to the wrong side of the related pieces according to the manufacturer's instructions. There are four Zipper Strip pieces, but fuse interfacing to only two of them.

Pocket

2 Bring the short sides of the POCKET together, right sides facing. Sew with a ¼" (6mm) seam allowance. Rotate the piece so the seam is down the center. Sew the top raw edge with a ¼" (6mm) seam allowance. (Fig. 1) Clip the corners and turn right side out. Topstitch the top edge at ¼" (6mm). Fold the lower edge in ¼" (6mm), wrong sides facing, and press. (Fig. 2)

Figure 1

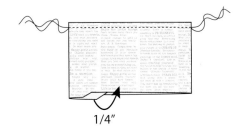

1/4"

Figure 2

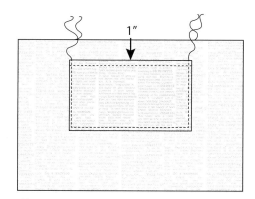

Figure 3

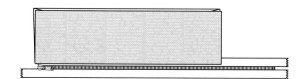

Figure 4

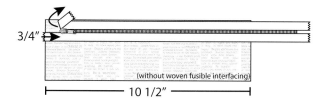

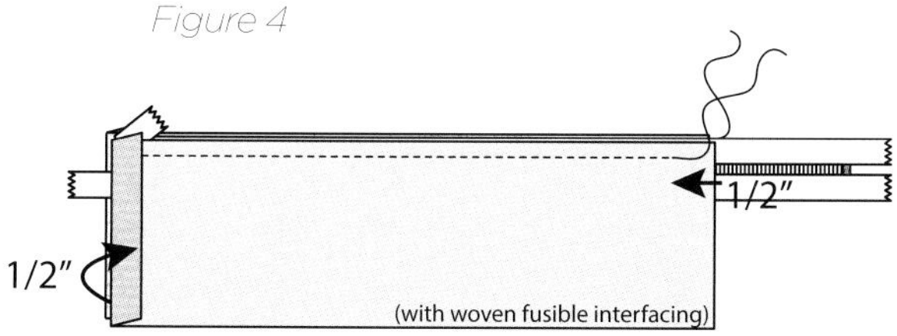

Figure 5

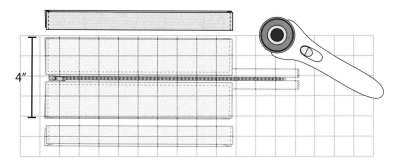

Figure 6

3 Position the Pocket centered and 1" (2.5cm) down from the upper edge of BODY LINING BOTTOM. Topstitch the Pocket sides and lower edge at ⅛" (3mm). This will close the opening left for turning. (Fig. 3)

Zipper Strip

4 Align the long side of one ZIPPER STRIP without interfacing with the zipper; the zipper pull should face away from the right side of the Zipper Strip. The teeth of the zipper should begin ¾" (2cm) from the edge of the Strip; the zipper end will extend beyond the piece. Fold the zipper tails at the top of the zipper up into the seam allowance. (Fig. 4) Align the Zipper Strip piece with another ZIPPER STRIP piece with interfacing, right sides facing. The zipper is sandwiched between two Zipper Strip layers.

5 Sew with a ¼" (6mm) seam allowance, beginning and ending ½" (1.3cm) from the edges of the Strip. The tails from the top of the zipper should be securely hidden in the seam allowance. Fold all the short ends of the Zipper Strips back ½" (1.3cm), wrong sides facing, and press. (Fig. 5)

6 Turn right-side out with wrong sides facing. Align both sides so the raw edges are hidden between the pieces. (Fig. 6) Topstitch both ends and along the zipper at ⅛" (3mm).

7 Repeat for the other side of the zipper using the remaining Zipper Strip pieces.

8 Trim the piece to a total width of 4" (10cm) with the zipper running down the center. (Fig. 7)

Figure 7

Zipper End

9 Press both short ends of ZIPPER END piece back ¼" (6mm), wrong sides facing. (Fig. 8) Fold in half, bringing the short ends together, right sides facing. Sew the sides with a ¼" (6mm) seam allowance. (Fig. 9) Clip the corners and turn right side out.

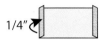

Figure 8

Figure 9

10 In the lower couple of inches (centimeters) of the zipper, fold the braid on the sides toward the back of the zipper and pin (see Fig. 10).

11 Slip this end of the zipper into the Zipper End piece. The Zipper End piece will be wider than the zipper. Topstitch closed at ⅛" (3mm). Repeat the topstitching a couple of times for reinforcement. (Fig. 10)

> Tip: Because there are so many thicknesses, pin on both sides of the zipper so they don't slip out of place. Also, use a strong sewing machine needle to get through all of the layers and zipper teeth.

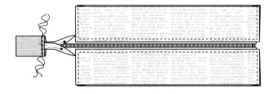

Figure 10

Assembling the Lining

12 Align one 11½" (29cm) side of the Body Bottom Lining with the BODY LINING TOP, right sides facing. Center the Zipper Strip between the two pieces with the zipper pull facing the Top Lining piece. The Lining pieces are longer than the Zipper Strip. (Fig. 11) Sew with a ½" (1.3cm) seam allowance. Topstitch the seam allowance to the Bottom Lining piece at ⅛" (3mm) (see Fig. 12).

13 Repeat for the remaining Body Lining pieces on the other side of the Zipper Strip. (Fig. 12)

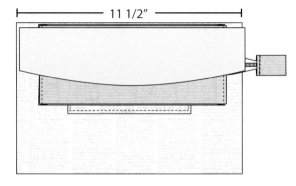

Figure 11

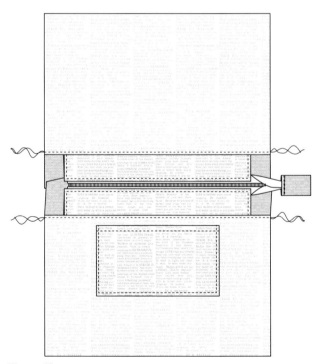

Figure 12

14 Align the lower edges of the Lining pieces together, right sides facing. Sew the lower seam with a ½" (1.3cm) seam allowance, but sew only 1" (2.5cm) on both ends. (Fig. 13) Press the seam open as if it were sewn all the way.

Tip: The large opening is for turning right-sides out and for inserting the Peltex.

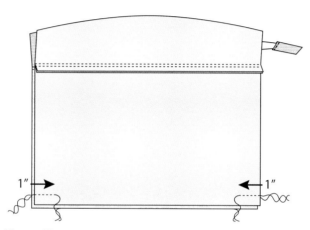

Figure 13

15 Align the SIDE LINING piece with the assembled Lining piece, right sides facing. The top edge of the Side piece will be ½" (1.3cm) above the Zipper Strip seam. Cut ⅜" (1cm) clips in the Body Lining raw edge to help it align smoothly with the curved corners of the Side piece.

Figure 14

16 Sew with a ½" (1.3cm) seam allowance beginning and ending ½" (1.3cm) from the top of the Side piece. (Fig. 14)

17 Repeat for the other Side piece.

18 Open the zipper and turn right-side out.

Handle Tabs

19 Press the long edges of the HANDLE TABS piece in ⅜" (1cm), wrong sides facing. Fold it in half lengthwise, wrong sides facing, and press. The finished width should be 1¼" (3.2cm). Topstitch both sides at ⅛" (3mm). (Fig. 15)

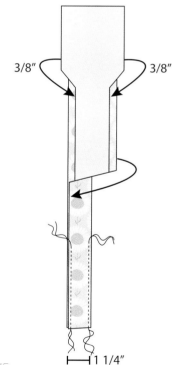

Figure 15

20 Cut the piece into four 4" (10cm) pieces. Slip one Tab piece through one O-ring and fold in half.

21 Place the outer edge of the Tab at 1¼" (3.2cm) in from the top corner of the Lining Body piece, right sides facing. Position the raw edges of the Tab ½" (1.3cm) above the Body edge. Baste at ¼" (6mm) three or four for extra reinforcement. (Fig. 16)

> Tip: Extending the Tab beyond the raw edge of the bag gives a little more protection from the edges fraying and coming out of the seam down the road.

22 Repeat for the other Tabs.

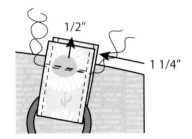

Figure 16

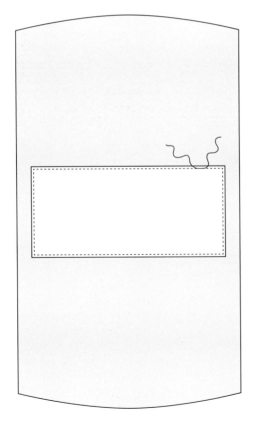

Figure 17

Assembling the Body

23 Center the Peltex on the EXTERIOR BODY piece wrong side. Topstitch the perimeter of the Peltex at ⅛" (3mm). (Fig. 17)

24 Align one EXTERIOR SIDE with the Exterior Body, right sides facing as shown. (Fig 18) The top edge of the Exterior Body piece will extend 1¼" (3.2cm) beyond the Exterior Side on both sides. Cut ⅜" (1cm) clips in the Body raw edge to help it align smoothly with the curved corners of the Side piece.
   Sew with a ½" (1.3cm) seam allowance, beginning and ending ½" (1.3cm) from the top of the Side piece. (Fig. 18)

Figure 18

25 Repeat for the remaining Side piece.

26 Set the Lining inside the Exterior, aligning the Body and Side raw edges. Sew the Lining and Exterior sides and body pieces together with a ½" (1.3cm) seam allowance from the seam beginning and ending points from steps 16 and 24. (Fig. 19) Move the seam allowance from the previous seams out of the way to do this.

> Tip: This is done in four separate seams: front, back, side left, side right. Use a small stitch length along the curved front and back. Shift the zipper out of the way as you sew these seams.

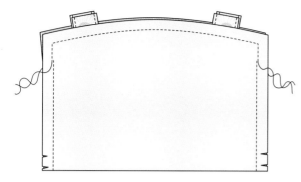

Figure 19

28 Trim the seam allowance in the top front and back curved pieces to ⅛" (3mm). Do not clip the Tab ends. Clip the corners. Turn right-side out through the Lining opening. Tuck the Lining inside the Exterior. Press the top edges flat.

28 Reaching inside through the Lining, push the side seam allowance toward the center front and back.

29 Topstitch the top of the two Side pieces at ½" (1.3cm), from seam to seam. This creates a casing for the elastic. Reaching inside through the lining, thread a 5" (12.5cm) piece of elastic through each casing. Leave ½" (1.3cm) of elastic extending beyond the raw edge on both ends.

30 From the right side, stitch in the ditch from the top of the Side piece down 2" (5cm) along the seam on all four corners. (Fig. 20)

Tip: Be sure the seams from the Exterior and Lining are aligned. This secures the elastic in place and creates a more secure fit for the Supporting Peltex pieces.

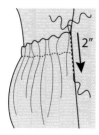

Figure 20

Magnets/Support Pieces

31 Trim ½" (1.3cm) off both sides of both BODY SUPPORT Peltex pieces. On the Peltex pieces, place four sew-in magnets along the top curved edges as shown and zigzag the perimeter several times. (Fig. 21)

Tip: To give added integrity to the vinyl covering the magnets, place a 1½" (3.8cm) piece of cotton over the magnet so it is sandwiched between two pieces of cotton when topstitched in place.

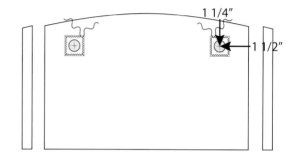

Figure 21

Tip: Place two negative magnets on the first Peltex piece and two positive magnets on the second piece. The magnetic pull should be away from the Peltex piece.

32 Through the opening in the Lining slip the Peltex piece with the positive magnets into the front of the purse between the Exterior and Lining Layers. The magnets will face toward the outside. Tuck the curve of the Peltex snuggly against the curve of the fabric, pulling all seam allowances toward the lining side of the purse. If the Peltex is too tight, trim a little off the edges. Once it is in place, pin the top portion through all layers, and pin the lower edge of the Peltex piece only to the Lining.

33 Pull the lower, recently pinned part of the lining out and away from the body of the purse, leaving the top of the Peltex tucked snugly in place. Topsitich the lower edge of the Peltex piece to the Lining at ⅛" (3mm). This is done through the opening in the Lining and, from the wrong side.

34 Do the same for the other Peltex piece on the back of the purse.

35 Close the Lining opening by blindstitching or topstitching. Tuck the Lining inside the Exterior.

Handle

36 Fold both ends of the HANDLE piece back ¼" (6mm), wrong sides facing, and press. Fold the Handle in half lengthwise, right sides facing. Sew the long seam with a ¼" (6mm) seam allowance. (Fig. 22) Attach a safety pin to one end at the seam. Thread the safety pin into the center of the sewn piece and guide it through to turn the piece right-side out.

37 Sew the end of a 12" (30.5cm) length of cording at ¼" (6mm) several times for reinforcement. Attach a safety pin to the cording, just past the stitching, and guide the cording into the Handle. (Fig. 23)

Tip: The fabric tube is snug against the cording, which makes threading tricky. Try putting a large safety pin or two onto the end of the fabric. This gives you something to hang onto when pulling the fabric down as the cording is pulled in the opposite direction.

38 When the end of the cording is 2¾" (7cm) past the top folded end of the Handle, secure the cording in place with a pin. The other end of the cording will be 2¾" (7cm) from the bottom folded end of the fabric. (Fig. 24)

Tip: The end of the cording will not quite reach the bottom of the Handle tube, so you will have to temporarily bunch the fabric up onto the cording so you can get the safety pin out. Once you have gotten the safety pin out, smooth the fabric along the cording.

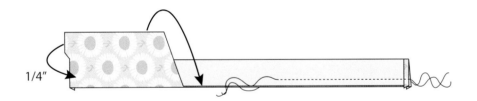

1/4"

Figure 22

Figure 23

1"

2 3/4"

Figure 24

39 Flatten the ends of the Handle tube so the seam is centered. Thread one end of the handle through one O-ring and fold 1" (2.5cm) back on itself, seam against seam. Tuck the corners of the fabric under to help hide the folded edge. Topstitch as shown. (Fig. 24) Repeat for the other end of the Handle.

40 Repeat for the remaining Handle. One handle is for the front of the bag. The other is for the back.

Changeable Cover

41 Buckle Strap, optional: Fold one short end of the CHANGEABLE COVER BUCKLE STRAP BOTTOM over ¼" (6mm), wrong sides facing, and press. Fold both long sides of the Buckle Strap Bottom over ¾" (2cm), wrong sides facing, and press. The finished width should be 1" (2.5cm). (Fig. 25)

42 Sew a ¼" (6mm) buttonhole centered 1¾" (4.5cm) down from the folded end. Thread the buckle through. Slide the catch of the buckle through the buttonhole and fold over the post 1¾" (4.5cm), wrong sides facing. Topstitch in place at ⅛" (3mm). (Fig. 26)

Tip: Make sure all raw edges are hidden, and when the buckle lays flat, make sure the catch is in the up position.

43 Fold the CHANGEABLE COVER BUCKLE STRAP TOP in half lengthwise, right sides facing. Sew with a ¼" (6mm) seam allowance. (Fig. 27) Position the seam down the center. Sew a diagonal at one end. Clip the corners and trim the diagonal seam allowance to ⅛" (3mm). (Fig. 28) Turn right-side out. Topstitch both sides and the diagonal end at ⅛" (3mm). Install an eyelet centered 4" (10cm) from the diagonal. (Fig. 29)

Tip: See page 15 for more on turning narrow pieces right-side out.

44 Thread the diagonal end through the buckle and latch. Pull the pieces taut. Place the strap 2½" (6.5cm) from the left edge of the CHANGEABLE COVER OUTSIDE as shown. (Fig. 30)

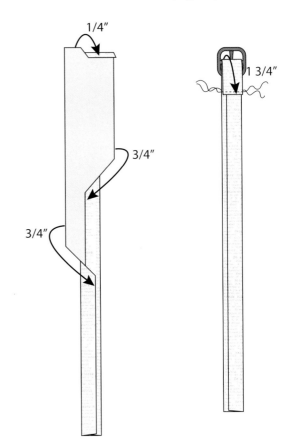

1/4"

1 3/4"

3/4"

3/4"

Figure 25　　　　　*Figure 26*

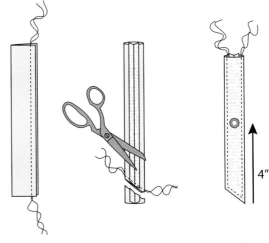

4"

Figure 27　　　*Figure 28*　　　*Figure 29*

45 Using the previous topstitching as a guide, topstitch the Strap Top piece along both sides to within ½" (1.3cm) of the buckle. Topstitch the Strap Bottom piece ⅛" (3mm) from both edges, up to the topstitching that holds the buckle in place. (Fig. 30) Trim off the overhanging portions.

46 To assemble the cover, fold the long straight edges of the CHANGEABLE COVER INSIDE FRONT/BACK pieces back ½" (1.3cm), wrong sides facing, and press. (Fig. 31) Align these two pieces with the Changeable Cover Outside ends, right sides facing.

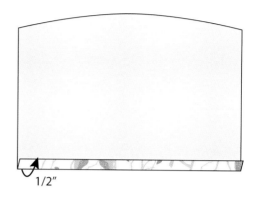

1/2"

Figure 31

2 1/2"

Figure 30

Center the CHANGEABLE COVER INSIDE BOTTOM piece to the middle of the Changeable Cover Outside, right sides facing. Sew the perimeter with a ½" (1.3cm) seam allowance. (Fig. 32) Trim the curved edges to a ⅛" (3mm) seam allowance. Clip the corners. Turn right-side out. Press the edges flat.

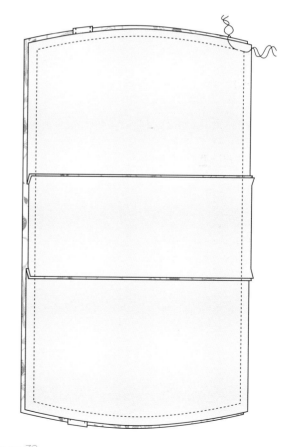

Figure 32

47 Center the SUPPORT BOTTOM (Peltex) piece behind the Inside Bottom piece. Install four purse feet as shown. (Fig. 33) Slip the purse feet prongs through the Outside and Peltex layers but not the Inside layer.

Tip: To give added integrity to the vinyl covering the magnets, place a 1½" (3.8cm) piece of cotton over the magnet so it is sandwiched between two pieces of cotton when topstitched in place.

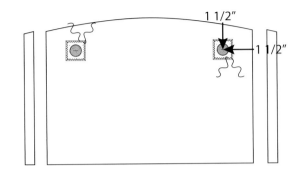

Figure 34

48 Trim off ½" (1.3cm) from the sides of both Body Peltex pieces. Make a mark 1½" (3.8cm) from the top and side edges, as shown. (Fig. 34) Install the magnets as in step 31.

Tip: Double-check that the space between the magnets is identical to the purse measurements. Before inserting the support into the Cover, double-check that the attraction will be perfect by putting the Peltex piece up to the purse.

49 Slip the Peltex piece with the negative magnets into the front and the piece with the positive magnets into the back of the Changeable Cover between the Outside and Inside layers. If the fit is too tight, trim a little off the sides of the Peltex. The magnets will face toward the back of the piece. Tuck it tightly into place by pulling all seam allowances toward the inside of the Cover.

50 Once the Peltex Support pieces are in place, pin the lower edge of the pieces. The fold of the Inside Front and Back pieces will overlap the raw edges of the Bottom piece. Topstitch ⅛" (3mm) from the pressed folds from step 46, catching all layers (Inside Front and Back, Inside Bottom and Outside) in the stitching. If the pieces are correct your topstitching will be in the groove between Peltex pieces. Snap the cover on the purse.

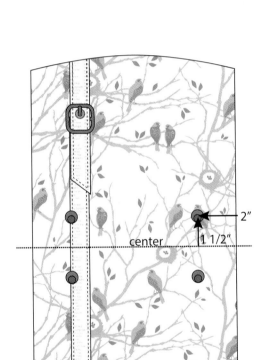

Figure 33

Lunch Date Clutch

This clutch takes fancy up a notch without sacrificing function. It brings pleats, lace, purse frames, metal hardware and zippers together for a sharp fashion statement. It is a clutch with a pocket for everything—all tucked into a small space. It easily opens at the center to allow access to credit cards and a window pocket for your ID. Both ends open to large pockets and a zipper-closing coin pocket as well. The removable, long shoulder strap allows for one-handed access, and all of this practicality is hidden behind a clean, feminine accent. You will live every day out of this clutch.

Size

10" wide × 6" tall × 1½" deep
(25.5cm × 15cm × 3.8cm)

Level of Difficulty (intermediate)

Fabric Choices

This clutch is perfect for using laminated cotton on the exterior. But if you choose laminated cotton or a heavy fabric, omit the pleats because they are too bulky for the frame. The interior is best with a quilting cotton or light-weight home décor fabric. Do not use laminated cotton on the interior. I recommend making the interior and exterior from the same fabric print because the interior is seen from the outside even when the clutch is closed. When choosing trim or lace, select something lightweight. Heavy trim may be too thick to fit into the purse frame. If you're drawn to thicker trim or lace, you can hand-sew it on after the frames have been glued.

Skills to Review

Gluing into Purse Frames *(page 18)*
Installing a Magnetic Snap Set (exterior application) *(page 18)*
Installing a Magnetic Snap Set (sew-in application) *(page 18)*
Sewing Laminated Cotton and Clear Vinyl *(page 16)*
Topstitching *(page 14)*

Materials

Yardage

½ yard (45.5cm) fabric for exterior

½ yard (45.5cm) fabric for interior

½ yard (45.5cm) fabric for lining

½ yard (45.5cm) fusible fleece

4¾" × 3½" (12cm × 9cm) piece of clear vinyl, 8 or 10 gauge

½ yard (45.5cm) per row lace/trim, 1½"– 2" (3.8cm–5cm) wide, optional

1" × 6" (2.5cm × 15cm) piece of Peltex

Hardware

2 sets of exterior magnets OR 3 sets of sew-in magnets (see Note on page 84)

2 purse frames, 3½" × 10" (9cm × 25.5cm)

2 swivel hooks, ¾" (2cm), optional

2 D-rings, ¾" (1.3cm), optional

Notions

Glue, such as Beacon 527 Multi-Use Glue

2 zippers, 7" (18cm)

Featured fabric by Lila Tueller of Lila Tueller Designs

Cutting

> Note: Measurements are given as width × length. See cutting charts on the CD, if desired.

From exterior fabric, cut:

1 rectangle 18" × 13½" (45.5cm × 34.5cm) for Body Exterior OR 1 rectangle 11½" × 13" (29cm × 33cm) if omitting pleats/lace

1 rectangle 2½" × 55" (6.5cm × 139.5cm) for Shoulder Strap. Note: This can be pieced.

2 rectangles 2½" × 3¼" (6.5cm × 8.5cm) for Shoulder Strap Tabs

From interior fabric, cut:

2 rectangles 14" × 6½" (35.5cm × 16.5cm) for Credit Card Pocket Strip

2 rectangles 3½" × 11½" (9cm × 29cm) for Credit Card Backing

2 rectangles 3½" × 4¾" (9cm × 12cm) for Window Pocket

1 Rectangle A 5" × 2½" (12.5cm × 6.5cm) for Center Interior Pocket Outside Top

1 Rectangle B 5" × 9½" (12.5cm × 24cm) for Center Interior Pocket Outside Bottom

2 Rectangle E 3" × 11½" (7.5cm × 29cm) for Interior Ends

From lining fabric, cut:

1 Rectangle C 5" × 2½" (12.5cm × 6.5cm) for Center Interior Pocket Inside Top

1 Rectangle D 5" × 17½" (12.5cm × 44.5cm) for Center Interior Pocket Inside Bottom

2 Rectangle F 11½" × 11" (29cm × 28cm) for Purse End Pockets

1 Rectangle G 9" × 8" (23cm × 20.5cm) for Coin Pocket

From fusible fleece, cut:

2 Rectangle E 4" × 11½" (10cm × 29cm) for Interior Ends

1 rectangle 11½" × 13" (29cm × 33cm) for Body Exterior

1 rectangle ¾" × 55" (2cm × 139.5cm) for Shoulder Strap. Note: This can be pieced.

From clear vinyl, cut:

1 rectangle 4¾" × 3½" (12cm × 9cm) for Window Pocket

From Peltex, cut:

4 squares 1" (2.5cm) for Interior Ends

Note on Magnets

When deciding between using standard exterior magnets and the invisible sew-in magnets, keep in mind that exterior magnets are more powerful and will keep the two sides of the clutch closed while it hangs from your shoulder—even when the clutch is a bit too full. But if the magnets are repeatedly yanked open, in time, the power of the magnets can pull the prongs through the fabric, even when the prongs are properly reinforced. The force can also pull the fabric out of the purse frame if pulled powerfully enough. Therefore, gently open the magnets with each use to protect the integrity of the fabric and the glue adhesion in the frame.

If sew-in magnets are chosen, do not overload the clutch, especially the front purse pocket. If it is too full, the clutch can pop open when jolted. The advantage to these magnets is that they close without being perfectly aligned.

When sewing sew-in magnets, place a 1½" (3.8cm) piece of cotton over the magnet so it is sandwiched between two pieces of cotton when topstitched in place. This will give added integrity to the vinyl covering the magnets.

Credit Card (CC) Pockets

1 Fold both CREDIT CARD POCKET STRIPS lengthwise, right sides facing, and sew the long edges with a ¼" (6mm) seam allowance. Turn right-side out and press flat. Topstitch the folded edge at ¼" (6mm). Cut each Strip into four pieces of 3½" (9cm) wide. (Fig. 1)

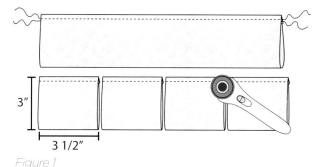

3"

3 1/2"

Figure 1

2 Align the top of one CC Pocket to one CREDIT CARD BACKING strip 2¾" (7cm) down from the top edge, right side. Topstitch the lower end of the CC Pocket at ⅛" (3mm). Place the second CC Pocket 1" (2.5cm) down from the previous pocket and topstitch the lower end at ⅛" (3mm). Repeat for a total of five CC Pockets on one CC Backing piece. Baste the long sides of the CC Backing with a ¼" (6mm) seam allowance. (Fig. 2)

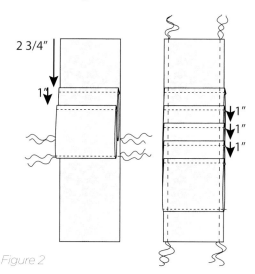

2 3/4"

1"

1"
1"
1"

Figure 2

3 Repeat step 2 with the remaining CC Backing strip and three CC Pockets, leaving space for the Window Pocket at the bottom. Do not baste yet.

Window Pocket

4 With the WINDOW POCKET fabric pieces right sides facing, topstitch a 1¾" × 3" (4.5cm × 7.5cm) rectangle centered (draw the rectangle on the fabric for convenience). Clip the center out to within ¼" (6mm) of the stitching. Clip into the corners. (Fig. 3) Turn right-side out and press the rectangle open.

5 Center the clear vinyl on the back of the Window Pocket and topstitch window opening at ⅛" (3mm). (Fig. 3) (See page 16 for tips on sewing clear vinyl.)

6 Fold the top and bottom raw edges (short edges) toward the wrong side ⅜" (1cm), hiding the edges between the fabric layers. Leave the vinyl extending beyond. (Fig. 3) Topstitch at ⅛" (3mm) along the top. Pin along the bottom. Trim the vinyl flush with the top and bottom folds.

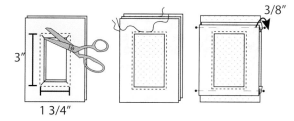

3/8"

3"

1 3/4"

Figure 3

7 Align the top of the Window Pocket 1" (2.5cm) down from the third CC Pocket. Topstitch the bottom at ⅛" (3mm) and again at ¼" (3mm).

8 Baste the sides of the CC Backing with a ¼" (6mm) seam allowance. (Fig. 4)

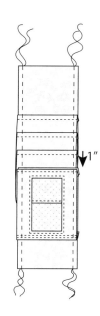

1"

Figure 4

Center Interior Pocket

9 Align the 5" (12.5cm) sides of RECTANGLE A and RECTANGLE C, right sides facing. Position one zipper between the two pieces with the zipper pull facing Rectangle A. Sew with a ¼" (6mm) seam allowance. Turn right-side out with wrong sides facing. Topstitch at ⅛" (3mm). (Fig. 5)

10 Repeat step 9 for RECTANGLE B and RECTANGLE D and the other side of the zipper. (Fig. 6)

11 Trim the excess zipper flush with the sides and whipstitch the end of the zipper, across the teeth. Bring the end of Rectangle D to the top of Rectangle C, right sides facing. (Fig. 7) Pin along both sides.

12 Evenly trim the excess off the top and bottom of the Center Pocket (Rectangles A and B) so the length is 11½" (29cm).

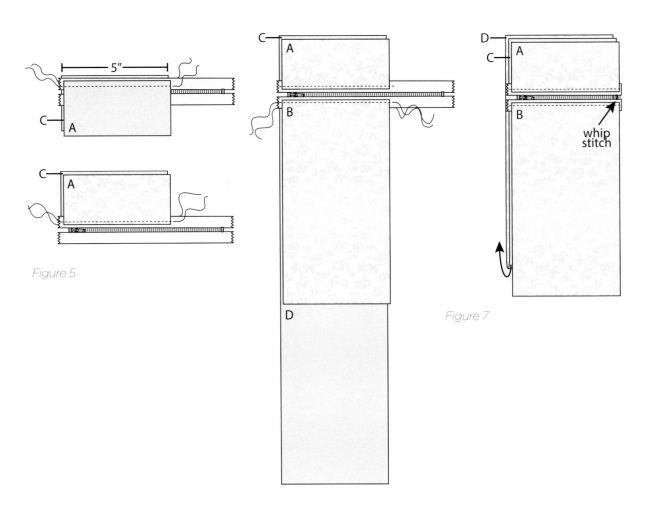

Figure 5

Figure 6

Figure 7

Assembling the Interior

13 Align the Center Interior Pocket with one CC Pocket piece, right sides facing. Sew with a ½" (1.3cm) seam allowance. Open out and press with seam allowance away from the CC Pocket piece. Top-stitch on the Center Interior Pocket side at ⅛" (3mm).

Tip: Topstitching over the zipper is a little bulky but doable.

14 Repeat for the other side of the Center Interior Pocket and remaining CC Pocket piece.

15 Align RECTANGLE E pieces with the other side of each CC Pocket piece, right sides facing, and sew with a ½" (1.3cm) seam allowance. Trim the seam allowance to ¼" (6mm). Open out and press with seam allowance away from the CC Pocket piece. Topstitch on the Rectangle E side at ⅛" (3mm).

16 Trim the piece to 13" × 11½" (33cm × 29cm). (Fig. 8)

17 Following the manufacturer's instructions, lightly fuse RECTANGLE E FUSIBLE FLEECE pieces to the wrong side of the ends of the assembled interior piece.

Tip: Be careful not to place the hot iron on the clear vinyl.

Magnets

If using sew-in magnets, skip this section.

18 On the Interior, make a mark at 2¾" (7cm) in from each side and 1⅜" (3.5cm) from the bottom edge. Repeat for the top of the interior. Install two sets of magnets (see page 18) at these locations. Be sure the magnets along the top are attracted to the corresponding ones along the bottom and that they line up perfectly. (Fig. 9)

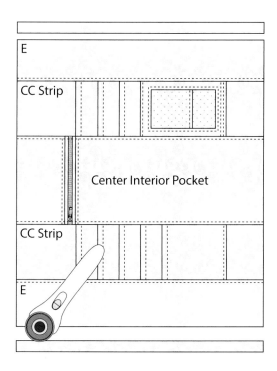

Figure 8

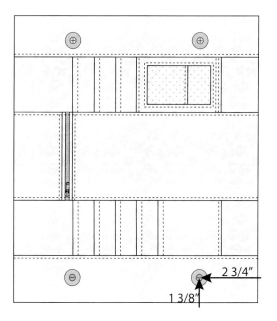

Figure 9

Purse End Pocket/Coin Pocket

19 Align one RECTANGLE F with RECTANGLE G, right sides facing, with long sides at the top. Center Rectangle G and place it ¾" (2cm) down from the top of Rectangle F. Draw a rectangle 7" × ½" (18cm × 1.3cm) on Rectangle G as shown. (Fig 10) Topstitch this drawn rectangle. Cut down the center of the sewn rectangle and into each corner, being careful not to clip through stitching. (Fig. 10) Insert the Pocket through the slit to the back side of the Rectangle and press flat to create a window slot.

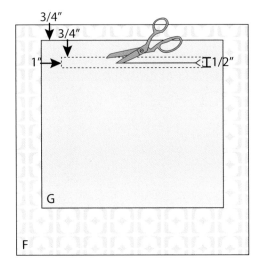

Figure 10

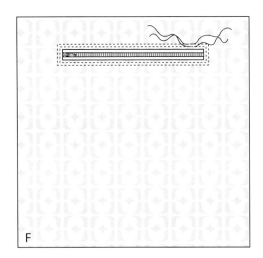

Figure 11

20 Center the second zipper in this opening. Extra zipper will extend beyond the opening on the inside. From the right side of Rectangle F, topstitch around the rectangle at ⅛" (3mm) and again at ¼" (6mm). (Fig. 11) Trim off the excess zipper, leaving a ½" (1.3cm) tail. Whipstitch across the teeth for strength.

21 From the wrong side of the work, fold the Rectangle G fabric in half, right sides facing. Moving Rectangle F out of the way, sew the three raw edges of Rectangle G with a ½" (1.3cm) seam allowance. (Fig. 12)

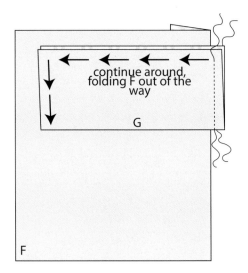

Figure 12

Alternate Sew-in Magnet Option

Skip this section if magnets are already installed.

22 Topstitch sew-in magnets to the wrong side of the Rectangle F's in the locations indicated. (Fig. 13) Topstitch around them a couple of times for added security. Be sure that the magnets attract to the related sides. The magnetic attraction should be up as it lays on the table; the wrong side of the fabric is also up.

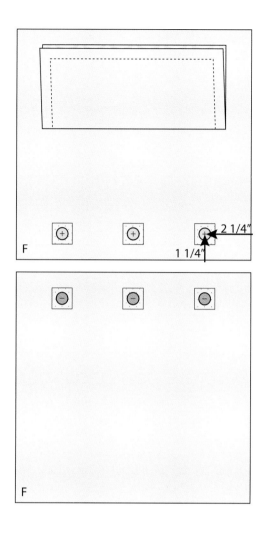

2 1/4″

1 1/4″

F

F

Figure 13

Tip: On the underside of the pleat, draw a line or adhere a piece of tape 1¼" (3.2cm) from the fold to guide the stitching line and ensure a straight seam. See page 14 for more topstitching tips.

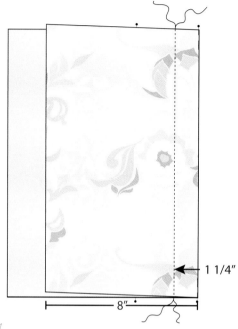

1 1/4″

8″

Figure 14

Pleats and Trim

If omitting pleats, skip to step 27.

23 Lay the BODY EXTERIOR piece right-side up with the short ends to the sides. Using pins, mark two vertical lines at 8" (20.5cm) and 11¼" (28.5cm) in from the left edge on the right side. Fold along each of these lines, wrong sides facing, and press. Topstitch 1¼" (3.2cm) from each of these folds. (Figs. 14 and 15)

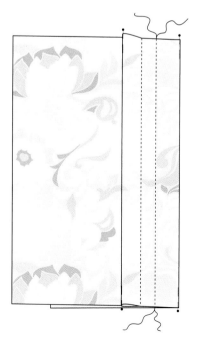

Figure 15

24 Press the pleats toward the right. (Fig. 16)

25 Under the pleats, position the lace/trim where preferred. Folding the pleats out of the way, topstitch the lace in place.

26 Trim the Body Exterior to 11½" × 13" (29cm × 33cm).

27 Fuse fusible fleece to the wrong side of the Body Exterior according to the manufacturer's instructions.

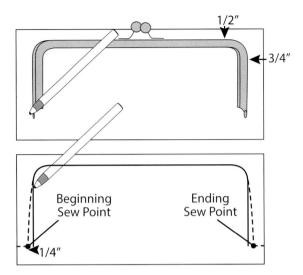

Figure 17

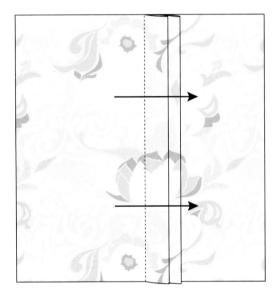

Figure 16

Body Assembling

28 Make a Template. Cut a piece of cardstock to 11½" × 5" (29cm × 12.5cm). Lay the purse frame over the rectangle as shown. (Fig. 17) Trace the shape of the frame. Mark a point ¼" (6mm) away from the bottom of the hinges. Draw lines from this mark to the top curve on both sides. These marks will be the beginning and ending sewing points. (Fig. 17) Make a clip in the cardstock from the outer edge to these beginning and ending sewing points. Cut along the drawn line. The outer portion of this piece is your template.

29 Align the end of Rectangle F with the end of the Interior that has the Window Pocket, right sides facing. Draw the outline of the template on this end of Rectangle F. (Fig. 18) Sew along the line from the beginning point to the ending point. Cut a ½" (1.3cm) clip through all layers of fabric from the raw edge to the beginning point; cut another clip to the ending point. Trim the Fusible Fleece away from the center of the piece so that only ½" (1.3cm) from the seamline remains."

The fusible fleece will be fused, so peel it away carefully so as not to stretch the fabric. Trim the seam allowance to ¼" (6mm) and clip the curved corners. (Fig. 19)

30 Repeat with the remaining Rectangle F and the other end of the Interior.

Alternate Instructions: If using sew-in magnets, sew the end of Rectangle F that has the magnets to the Interior piece.

31 Repeat with the Body Exterior and the free ends of Rectangles F. Omit the trimming of the fusible fleece for the two ends sewn to the Body Exterior. There will be a total of four of these curved seams.

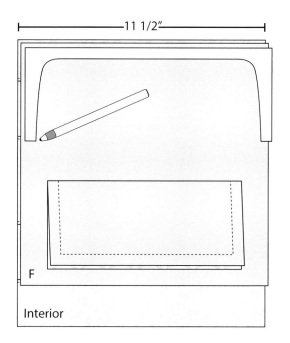

11 1/2"

F

Interior

Figure 18

32 Fold the body so the Purse End Pocket (Rectangle F) is folded in half, right sides facing. Expose the raw edges along the sides near the fold. Align the ½" (1.3cm) clips made in step 29 with each other. Sew with a ½" (1.3cm) seam allowance from the fold to the clips, being careful to fold the other body pieces out of the way. (Fig. 20) Repeat for each side of the purse pockets for a total of four seams.

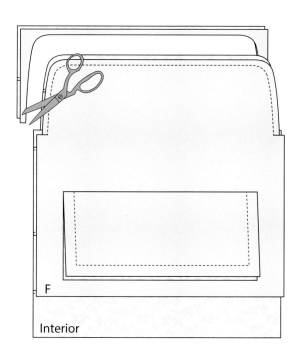

F

F

Interior

Figure 19

F

F

Exterior

Figure 20

33 Align the side raw edges of the Body Interior and Exterior pieces clip to clip, right sides facing. Sew the left side from clip to clip with a ½" (1.3cm) seam allowance. Sew the right side only ¾" (2cm) from each clip to leave an opening for turning. (Fig. 21) Turn right-side out. Blindstitch the opening closed.

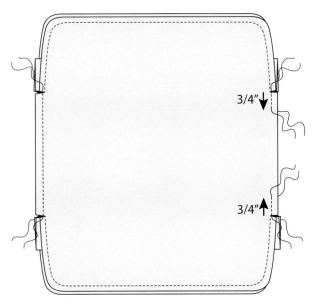

Figure 21

34 Topstitch all four purse ends at ⅛" (3mm), but start and stop 1" (2.5cm) from the beginning and end of the seams from step 33. Topstitch only in areas that will be glued into the frames.

Shoulder Strap and Tabs

35 Determine the desired length for the SHOULDER STRAP and trim off the extra length.

Alternate Instructions: If omitting the swivel hooks and D-rings, add 4" (10cm) to the desired length.

Cut the fusible fleece 1" (2.5cm) shorter than the Strap. Fuse the fusible fleece to the wrong side of the Strap so that it ends ½" (2.5 cm) from each short end and ½" (2.5 cm) in from the lower edge. Fold and press the Strap as illustrated. The finished width should be ¾" (2cm). Topstitch along both long edges at ⅛" (3mm). All raw edges should be hidden. (Fig. 22)

Alternate Instructions: If omitting the swivel hooks and D-rings, attach the Strap ends to the back of the Exterior body—through the end of the Strap, Body Exterior and one layer of the Purse End Pocket—by topstitching a ⅝" (1.5cm) square through the end of the Strap, no closer than ¾" (2cm) from the purse top or sides so it will not be in the way of gluing the purse into the frames. Because the Strap is thicker than the Tabs, it is too bulky for the magnets to secure if it is on the inside of the clutch. Skip to step 40.

36 Fold and press both ends and the long sides of the SHOULDER STRAP TABS as illustrated. All raw edges should be hidden, and the finished width should be ¾" (2cm). Topstitch both sides at ⅛" (3mm). Repeat for the other Tab. (Fig. 23)

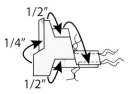

Figure 23

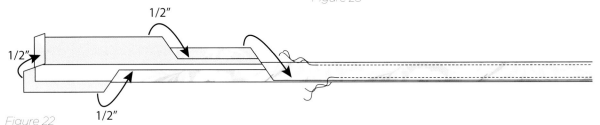

Figure 22

37 Attach the Shoulder Strap to the swivel hooks and Tabs to the D-rings as shown. (Figs. 24 and 25) Thread the ends through the hardware and fold over ¾" (2cm). Topstitch at ⅛" (3mm) several times for reinforcement and to catch all raw edges.

38 Pin a Tab's back side against the right side of the assembled Interior with the bottom of the Tab even with the seam for the CC Pocket and ⅝" (1.5cm) in from the side. (Fig. 24)

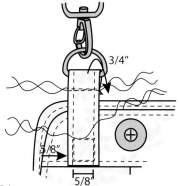

Figure 24

39 Attach the Tabs to the Interior—through the Interior layers and one layer of the Purse End Pocket—by topstitching the lower edge of the Tabs in a ⅝" (1.5cm) square as shown. (Fig 24) Repeat the topstitching several times for reinforcement.

Tip: The Tabs can comfortably fit inside the clutch when the Strap is not attached.

Glue into the Frames

40 Follow the instructions on page 18. Be careful to prop the tabs out of the way. The pleated/lace areas are a little difficult due to the added bulk. Push these edges inside the frame as far as the rest of the clutch so the line along the top will remain even.

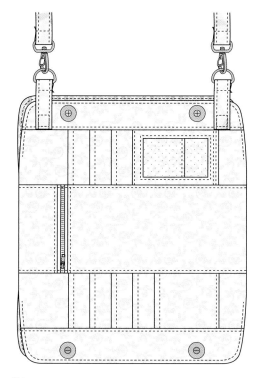

Figure 25

Double-Take Clutch

This clutch can add a feminine and romantic touch to your date night apparel. The adjustable strap with buckle and eyelets is not only a great accent, but it also allows for versatility. Lengthen the strap to pull across your body for a clutch that holds everything or just a tablet. Shorten the strap to hang from the shoulder, and add a couple of embellishments to create a personal fashion statement. The back zipper pocket is perfect for quick access to a mobile phone. The clutch is designed with optional hardware for the beginning sewer.

Size

10" wide × 6" tall × 1" deep
(25.5cm × 15cm × 2.5cm)

Level of Difficulty (beginner)

Fabric Choices

This pattern is designed to be a simple introduction to sewing on laminated cotton, but any home decor weight fabric, corduroy or twill will work for the exterior as well. Quilting cotton is best for the lining.

Skills to Review

Installing Eyelets/Grommets (page 18)
Sewing and Clipping Curves (page 14)
Sewing Laminated Cotton and Clear Vinyl (page 16)
Topstitching (page 14)

Materials

Yardage

½ yard (45.5cm) fabric for exterior

⅓ yard (30.5cm) fabric for lining

⅓ yard (30.5cm) fusible fleece

Hardware

1 metal center post buckle, ¾" (2cm), optional

2 metal rectangles, ¾" (2cm), optional

3 eyelet sets, ¼" (6mm), optional

Notions

1 sport zipper, 7" (18cm)

1 sport zipper, 9" (23cm)

Patterns

Double-Take Clutch patterns: Butterfly Body, Butterfly Wing (on CD)

Featured fabric by Chelsea Andersen of Pink Fig Design (floral) and Amanda Herring of The Quilted Fish (pink)

Cutting

> Note: Measurements are given as width × length. See cutting charts on the CD, if desired.

From exterior fabric, cut:

1 rectangle 11" × 25" (28cm × 63.5cm) for Body Exterior

1 rectangle 2¼" × 60" (5.5cm × 152.5cm) for Shoulder Strap. Note: This can be pieced.

1 rectangle 2¼" × 8" (5.5cm × 20.5cm) for Buckle Strap if adding hardware

2 rectangles 2¼" × 5" (5.5cm × 12.5cm) for Tabs if adding hardware

From lining fabric, cut:

2 rectangles 11" × 12½" (28cm × 31.5cm) for Body Lining

1 rectangle 9" × 10" (23cm × 25.5cm) for Pocket

From fusible fleece, cut:

1 rectangle 11" × 25"(28cm × 63.5cm) for Body

1 rectangle ¾" × 60" (2cm × 152.5cm) for Shoulder Strap. Note: This can be pieced.

1 rectangle ¾" × 7" (2cm × 18cm) for Buckle Strap if adding hardware

2 rectangles ¾" × 5" (2cm × 12.5cm) for Tabs if adding hardware

Pocket

1 Lay the BODY EXTERIOR and POCKET pieces with the short sides up, right sides facing. Position the Pocket top edge 6½" (16.5cm) down from the top edge of the Body and centered. On the wrong side of the Pocket, draw a rectangle 7¼" × ⅝" (18.5cm × 1.5cm) as shown. (Fig. 1)

2 Topstitch along the rectangle. Cut down the center of the sewn rectangle and into each corner, being careful not to clip the stitching. (Fig. 1) Insert the Pocket piece through the slit to the wrong side of the Exterior and press around the opening, creating a finished window slot.

Figure 1

3 Center the 7" (18cm) zipper on the inside of the pocket through the opening. Topstitch at ⅛" (3mm) and again at ¼" (6mm). (Fig. 2)

Figure 2

4 On the back side, fold the Pocket fabric in half, bringing the short ends together, right sides facing. Folding the Body out of the way, sew the three raw edges of the Pocket with a ½" (1.3cm) seam allowance. (Fig. 3)

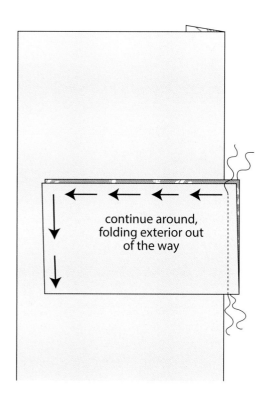

continue around, folding exterior out of the way

Figure 3

5 According to the manufacturer's instructions, fuse fusible fleece to the wrong side of the Body Exterior.

Tabs

6 Fuse fusible fleece to the TABS (or SHOULDER STRAP) ⅜" (1cm) in from one long edge on the wrong side, following the manufacturer's instructions.

7 Press the long sides over ⅜" (1cm), wrong sides facing. Fold in half lengthwise and press. The finished width should be ¾" (2cm). Topstitch along both long edges at ⅛" (3mm). (Fig. 4)

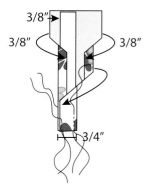

3/8"
3/8"
3/8"
3/4"

Figure 4

8 Thread each tab through a metal rectangle, fold in half and pin closed.

Alternate instructions: If omitting the hardware, follow steps 6–7 using the SHOULDER STRAP piece. Then determine the desired length of the strap, add 1" (2.5cm) and trim.

9 Position the raw edges of the Tabs/Strap 5½" (14cm) down from the top edge of the Body Exterior on the right side. Baste in place with a ½" (1.3cm) seam allowance (see Fig. 5).

Zipper Opening

10 Center the 9" (23cm) zipper with the top edge of the Body Exterior, right sides facing. Sew with a ¼" (6mm) seam allowance, beginning and ending 1" (2.5cm) from the edge. Do not sew the tails of the zipper. (Fig. 5) Center the other side of the zipper on the remaining end of the Body Exterior, right sides facing, and sew along the zipper teeth in the same way. You should now have a loop with each end of the Body Exterior sewn to the 9" (23cm) zipper tape.

11 Fold the zipper tails away as shown. (Fig. 6) Along the top edge of the Body Exterior, align one 11" (28cm) edge of the Body Lining, with the Zipper between them, right sides facing along the seam allowance as shown. Sew with a ¼" (6mm) seam allowance, beginning and ending 1" (2.5cm) from the side edges as before. (Fig. 7)

12 Repeat with the other side of the zipper and the remaining Lining piece.

13 Turn right-side out. Align the Lining and Exterior, wrong sides facing. Topstitch both sides of the zipper at ⅛" (3mm) and again at ¼" (6mm), beginning and ending 1" (2.5cm) from the raw ends.

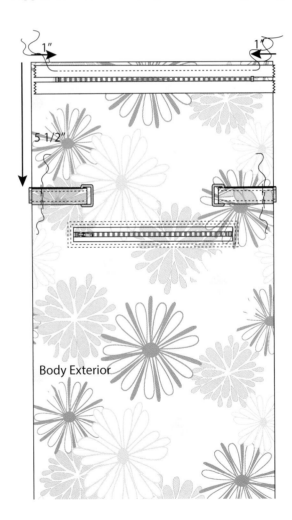

Figure 5

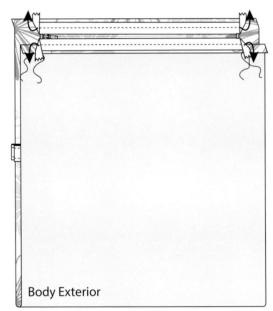

Figure 6

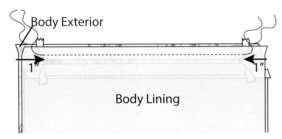

Figure 7

Finishing the Body

14 Turn wrong-side out pulling the Lining and Exterior away from each other. Fold the Exterior in half so it is right sides facing with itself and aligning the raw edges. Fold back the raw edges that are in the zipper seam ¼" (6mm), wrong sides facing as shown. (Fig. 8) This will create an even fold from the zipper all the way to the edge. (This is the 1" [2.5cm] area that has not been sewn in steps 10–13.) Sew the two sides of the Exterior with a ½" (1.3cm) seam allowance. (Fig. 8) Backstitch several times in the center where the Tabs or Straps are for extra security. Clip the lower corners. Trim away the fusible fleece in the seam allowance.

> Tip: Be careful not to catch the Shoulder Strap in the seam allowance if sewing without the hardware.

15 Fold the Lining in half so it is right sides facing with itself and aligning the raw edges. Fold back the raw edges that are in the zipper seam ¼" (6mm), wrong sides facing as shown. (Fig. 8) This will create an even fold from the zipper all the way to the edge. (This is the 1" [2.5cm] area that has not been sewn in steps 12–13.) Sew both side seams of the Lining. At the beginning, near the zipper, the seam allowance is ½" (1.3cm), but gradually increase it to ¾" (2cm) seam allowance in the first 2" (5cm) of the seam. (Fig. 8)

> Tip: With lining smaller it will fit more neatly inside the Exterior.

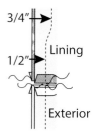

Figure 8

16 Turn right-side out through the Lining opening. Tuck the Lining inside the Exterior. At the top where the zipper opens, fold the seam allowance of both the Exterior and Lining open and flat. Topstitch from front to back, completing the topstitching from step 13.

17 Pull the Lining back out. Fold the lower edges in ½" (6mm), wrong sides facing and pin. Align these folds (Front and Back) of the Lining with each other and topstitch closed at ⅛" (3mm). Tuck the Lining back inside the Exterior."

Buckle Strap

Skip this section if omitting the hardware.

18 Fuse fusible fleece to the wrong side of the BUCKLE STRAP ⅜" (1cm) away from the long edge and ½" (1.3cm) away from both ends, according to the manufacturer's instructions. Fold the ends over ½" (1.3cm), wrong sides facing, and press.

Press the long sides over ⅜" (1cm), wrong sides facing. Fold in half lengthwise and press. The finished width should be ¾" (2cm). Be sure all the raw edges are tucked inside. Topstitch along both long edges at ⅛" (3mm). (Fig. 9)

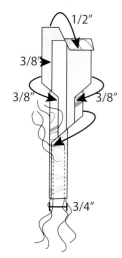

Figure 9

> Tip: Pressing on laminated cotton will likely not lay the material flat, but it will leave a fold that can be used as a guide. Always use a pressing cloth.

19 Sew a ¼" (6mm) buttonhole centered 1" (2.5cm) down from one end. For laminated cotton, you do not need to sew a buttonhole; you need to make only a ¼" (6mm) cut because the fabric will not fray. Thread this end through the buckle. Slide the catch of the buckle through the buttonhole and fold over the post 1" (2.5cm). Topstitch in place at ⅛" (3mm) several times for reinforcement. (Fig. 10)

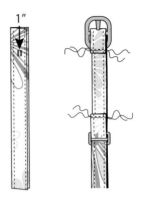

Figure 10

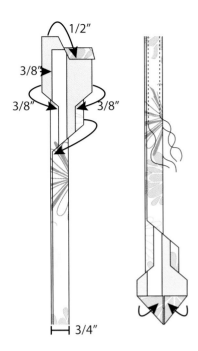

Figure 11

20 Thread the other end of the Buckle Strap through one of the rectangles on a Tab. Fold over 1" (2.4cm). The buckle should face outward and the folds should face inward when the purse is worn. Topstitch closed at ⅛" (3mm). (Fig. 10)

Shoulder Strap

Skip this section if omitting the hardware.

21 Determine the desired length of the Strap by measuring from the buckle to the other rectangle and adding 13" (33cm). Trim the SHOULDER STRAP to that length. Trim the fusible fleece 1¼" (3.2cm) shorter than that length.

22 Following the manufacturer's instructions, fuse fusible fleece to the wrong side of the Shoulder Strap ⅜" (1cm) in from one long edge and ½" (1.3cm) down from one end (this will be the flat end) and ¾" (2cm) up from the other end (this will be the pointed end).

23 Press the flat end over ½" (1.3cm), wrong side facing. Press both long edges in ⅜" (1cm), wrong sides facing. Fold in half lengthwise and press. The finished width should be ¾" (2cm). Open the pointed end. Press this end up ½" (1.3cm), wrong

sides facing. Press both corners up to the center fold, creating 45-degree angles. Refold the sides and fold in half again. The result will be a pointed end with all the raw edges hidden. (Fig. 11)

24 Topstitch the entire Strap perimeter at ⅛" (3mm).

25 Thread the square end of the Shoulder Strap piece through the other metal rectangle. Fold the end over 1" (2.5cm). Be sure the folds are inward as the clutch will be worn. Topstitch at ⅛" (3mm) to secure.

26 Thread the angled end of the Strap through the buckle. Install eyelets (see page 18) at the desired locations, about 1¼" (3.2cm) apart.

Butterfly

27 Align two 4" (10cm) squares of laminated cotton, wrong sides facing. Pin two wing patterns on the laminate, leaving at least ½" (1.3cm) space between the wings. Using the pattern as a guide, stitch around the edge of the pattern. (See page 14 for Sewing and Clipping Curves.) Remove the paper pattern. Trim around the wings ⅛" (3mm) away from the stitching.

28 Fuse a 2" (5cm) square of Peltex to the wrong side of a 2" (5cm) square of laminated cotton. Pin one Body pattern on the laminate. Using the pattern as a guide, stitch around the edge of the pattern. Remove the paper pattern. Trim around the body ⅛" (3mm) away from the stitching.

Tip: Use silk pins to minimize holes in the laminate.

29 Fold the wing in half, bringing the points together. Sew a line as shown. (Fig. 12) Open the wing up. Fold the triangle portion that was just sewn so it will lay against itself on the back side. This creates a cupping shape. Align the tip of the sewn triangle to the center of the Butterfly Body piece along the straight edge. This triangle portion will lay along the straight edge of the Body and there will be a curved portion of the Wing, the unsewn edge, that will stick out from the center of the Body. Prepare the other wing similarly but mirrored for the other side of the body.

30 You can adjust the angle of the wings a little for a more natural position. Topstitch a small ½" (1.3cm) line near the seams to secure the wings to the body.

31 Tack or pin the butterfly in place on the flap of the clutch.

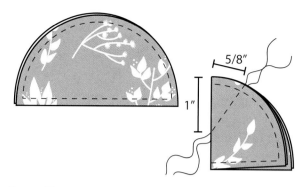

Figure 12

Be Creative

When you throw the strap over your shoulder, the zipper end will naturally fold over. With the pocket zipper against you, the other half of the clutch is the front. Stitch an embellishment, such as jewelry, a knitted rose or a fabric butterfly, onto the front. Or better yet, pin something on so it can be changed often. Remember to use silk pins to limit permanent punctures on laminated cotton.

Day-by-Day Wallet

The *Day-by-Day Wallet* is a go-to piece for the woman who wants to be organized throughout the day but still likes to look spontaneously creative. Are you kidding? A ruffle on your wallet? Invisible magnets keep it magically closed. There are credit card holders, a clear ID holder and two roomy, clear vinyl zippered pages to hold everything else. It is darling coming out of your purse or hanging from your wrist as a small clutch. Once you make one, you will not be able to resist making one in every color. Give it a whirl.

Size

4½" wide × 9" tall × 1¼" deep
(11.5cm × 23cm × 3.2cm)

Level of Difficulty (intermediate)

Fabric Choices

This wallet is perfect for a laminated cotton exterior. If you choose to use quilting cotton for the exterior, reinforce it with woven fusible interfacing for both the body piece and the wrist strap. The interior is best with quilting cotton or lightweight home décor fabric; do not use laminated cotton on the interior. The ruffle is best made of laminated cotton. You can use quilting cotton, but the edges will fray, which is a cute look, too. You can also cut the cotton edges with pinking shears.

Skills to Review

Installing a Magnetic Snap Set (sew-in application)
(page 18)
Sewing and Clipping Curves (page 14)
Sewing Laminated Cotton and Clear Vinyl (page 16)
Topstitching (page 14)
Working with Peltex (page 15)

Materials

Yardage

⅓ yard (30.5cm) fabric for exterior

½ yard (45.5cm) fabric for interior

16" × 10" (40.5cm × 25.5cm) piece of fusible fleece

4¾" × 3½" (12cm × 9cm) and 18" × 8" (45.5cm × 20.5cm) pieces of clear vinyl, 8- or 10-gauge

2" × 8¾" (5cm × 22cm) and 9" × 4" (23cm × 10cm) pieces of Peltex

40" × 1½" (101.5cm × 3.8cm) piece of fabric for ruffle, optional

Hardware

2 sets of invisible sew-in magnets

Notions

2 zippers, 7" (18cm)

1 sport zipper, 7" (18cm)

2 yards (1.8m) double-fold bias tape, ¼" (6mm)

Patterns

Day-by-Day Wallet patterns: End Support, Exterior Curve Template, Corner Template (on CD)

Cutting

> Note: Measurements are given as width × length. See cutting charts on the CD, if desired.

From exterior fabric, cut:

1 rectangle 15½" × 10" (39.5cm × 25.5cm) for Exterior Body

1 rectangle 40" × 1½" (101.5cm × 3.8cm), for optional Ruffle. Note: This can be pieced.

1 rectangle 2" × 14" (5cm × 35.5cm) for Wrist Strap

From interior fabric, cut:

2 rectangles 14" × 6½" (35.5cm × 16.5cm) for Credit Card Pocket Strip

2 rectangles 3½" × 10" (9cm × 25.5cm) for Credit Card Backing

2 rectangles 3½" × 4¾" (9cm × 12cm) for Window Pocket

1 Rectangle A 4" × 10" (10cm × 25.5cm) for Center Panel

1 Rectangle B 1½" × 10" (3.8cm × 25.5cm) for Left Panel

1 Rectangle C 7" × 10" (18cm × 25.5cm) for Right Panel

1 rectangle 10" × 8½" (25.5cm × 21.5cm) for Zipper Pocket

From fusible fleece, cut:

1 rectangle 15½" × 10" (39.5cm × 25.5cm) for Body

From larger piece of clear vinyl, cut:

1 rectangle 4¾" × 3½" for Window Pocket

2 rectangles 8½" × 7¾" (21.5cm × 19.5cm) for Clear Vinyl Pages

From Peltex, cut:

2 rectangles 1" × 8¾" (2.5cm × 22cm) for Center Panel

1 End Support from pattern

Note

Illustrations do not show ruffle option.

Note

At the end of the project, you will be topstitching on the laminated cotton. Use a longer stitch for a cleaner look. Determine a topstitching length (3 to 3.5) from the beginning and use that size stitch for all the topstitching, even on the cotton interior. Don't use it, however, on the clear vinyl insert pages; they have curves that require a small stitch to look neat.

Credit Card (CC) Pockets

1 Fold both CREDIT CARD POCKET STRIPS lengthwise, right sides facing, and sew the long edges with a ¼" (6mm) seam allowance. Turn right-side out. Topstitch the folded edge at ¼" (6mm). Cut each Strip into four pieces 3½" (9cm) wide. (Fig. 1)

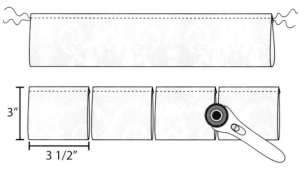

Figure 1

2 Align the top of one CC Pocket to the right side of one CREDIT CARD BACKING 2" (5cm) down from the top edge. Topstitch the lower end of the CC Pocket at ⅛" (3mm). Place the second CC Pocket 1" (2.5cm) down from the previous pocket and topstitch the lower end at ⅛" (3mm). Repeat for a total of five CC Pockets. Baste the long sides of CC Backing with a ¼" (6mm) seam allowance. (Fig. 2)

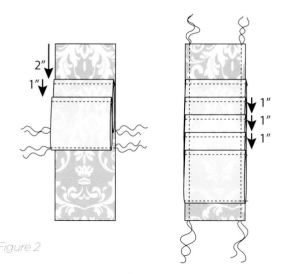

Figure 2

3 Repeat step 2 with the remaining CC Backing strip and three CC pockets, leaving space for the Window Pocket at the bottom. Do not baste yet.

Window Pocket

4 Draw a 1¾" × 3" (4.5cm × 7.5cm) rectangle in the center of one WINDOW CREDIT CARD POCKET. Align the two Window CC Pockets, right sides facing, and topstitch the rectangle. Clip the center out to within ¼" (6mm) of the stitching. Clip into the corners, being careful not to clip through the stitching. (Fig. 3) Turn right-side out. Press the rectangle open.

5 Center the small rectangle of clear vinyl to the back of the Window Pocket and topstitch around the inner rectangle at ⅛" (3mm). (Fig. 3) (See page 16 for more on sewing laminated cotton and clear vinyl.)

6 Fold the top and bottom (short) raw edges toward the wrong side ⅜" (1cm), hiding the edges between the cotton layers. Leave the clear vinyl extending beyond. (Fig. 3) Topstitch at ⅛" (3mm) along the top. Pin along the bottom. Trim the clear vinyl flush with the top and bottom folds.

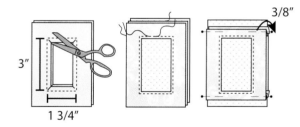

Figure 3

7 Align the top of the Window Pocket 1" (2.5cm) down from the third CC Pocket. Topstitch the bottom at ⅛" (3mm) and again at ¼" (6mm). Baste the sides of CC Backing with a ¼" (6mm) seam allowance. (Fig. 4)

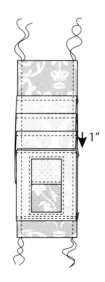

Figure 4

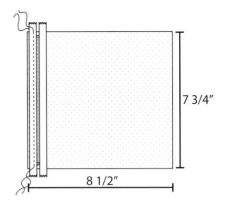

7 3/4″

8 1/2″

Figure 5

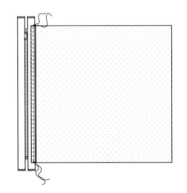

Figure 6

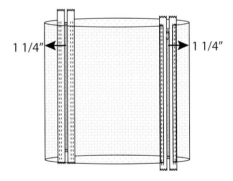

1 1/4″   1 1/4″

Figure 7

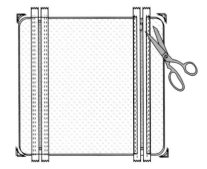

Figure 8

Clear Vinyl Insert Pages

8 Lay one edge of one regular 7″ (18cm) zipper tape facedown along the 7¾″ (19.5cm) edge of one CLEAR VINYL PAGE. Sew with a ¼″ (6mm) seam allowance. (Fig. 5) Open with the right sides up and topstitch at ⅛″ (3mm). (Fig. 6) Repeat sewing the other half of the zipper tape to the remaining Clear Vinyl Page.

9 Repeat the previous step using the free ends of the Clear Vinyl Pages and remaining regular 7″ (18cm) zipper. Be sure both zipper pulls are at the top. When done, the two clear vinyl pieces will create a cylinder. (Fig. 7)

Tip: Topstitching the last zipper is tricky. It helps if you open both zippers because this will give you a little more room in which to work. Also, keep the two zippers open when turning the cylinder right-side out to prevent crushing the clear vinyl. (Fig. 7)

10 Fold the clear vinyl cylinder as shown with the right-hand zipper facing up and the left-hand zipper facing down. (Fig. 7)

11 Lay the piece flat and work out any bubbles. Use the Corner Template to cut a curved edge on all four corners of flattened Clear Vinyl Page. (Fig. 8)

12 Open the double-fold bias tape. Starting at the center bottom of the clear vinyl, position the edges of the clear vinyl inside the bias tape, all the way to the bias tape fold, and then refold the bias tape. Pin around the perimeter, smoothing the curves without pulling the bias tape tightly. Be careful with

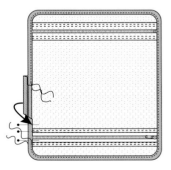

Figure 9

your pins (see more on pinning clear vinyl on page 16). Overlap the ends of the bias tape about ¼" (6mm).

13 Using a smallish stitch length, topstitch the bias tape at ⅛" (3mm). (Fig. 9)

Assembling the Interior

14 Assemble the interior in the order shown (see Fig. 10). Sew all seams, right sides facing, with a ½" (1.3cm) seam allowance. Trim the seam allowance for Rectangle B and the CC Strip to ¼" (6mm). Topstitch all seams on the rectangle side at ⅛" (3mm) with the seam allowances folded away from the CC Pocket Strips. (Fig. 10)

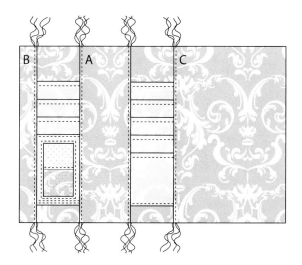

Figure 10

15 According to the manufacturer's instructions, fuse one 1" (2.5cm) Peltex piece to the center of Rectangle A on the wrong side (see Fig. 12).

16 Align the Clear Vinyl Page with the right side of the Interior with the zipper pulls at the top. Match the vertical centers of the Clear Vinyl Page and Rectangle A. The page will be about 1" (2.5cm) from the top and bottom.
    Topstitch down the center, attaching the Peltex, Interior and Clear Vinyl Page. Topstitch again ¼" (6mm) from both sides of the previous stitching. (Fig. 11)

> Tip: The center stitching hides the holes made by the pins used to align the Clear Vinyl Page to the Interior. The second and third sets of stitching keep the pages separated for practical use when the wallet is finished.

17 According to the manufacturer's instructions, fuse the other 1" (2.5cm) Peltex piece 4¾" (12cm) from the previous Peltex piece on the wrong side. (Fig. 12)

> Tip: If the Peltex doesn't adhere, put a couple of pins on the right side of the fabric to hold it in place.

18 The outer dimensions should be 15½" × 10" (39.5cm × 25.5cm). Trim to square up the piece if needed.

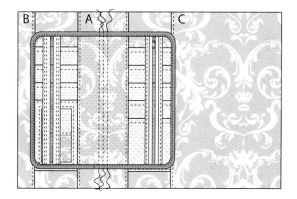

Figure 11

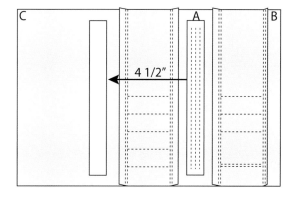

Figure 12

Wrist Strap

19 Fold both long sides of the WRIST STRAP as shown and press. Topstitch both sides at ⅛" (3mm). (Fig. 13)

20 Fold the Strap in half, making a loop. Align the raw edges of the Strap with the top center of Rectangle A, right sides facing. Baste in place at ¼" (6mm) several times for security.

Shaping the Body Pieces

21 Lay the Exterior Curve Template over Rectangle C and cut. Using the Corner Template, cut both corners from Rectangle B. Do the same for the EXTERIOR BODY and FF pieces. (Fig. 14)

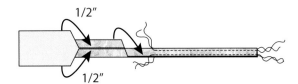

Figure 13

> Tip: I put the two ends at a slight angle to each other so they open a little separated when resting on a table (see Fig. 21 on page 112).

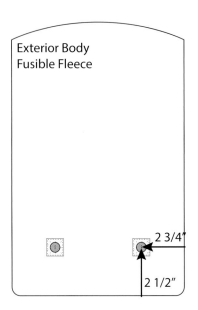

Figure 15

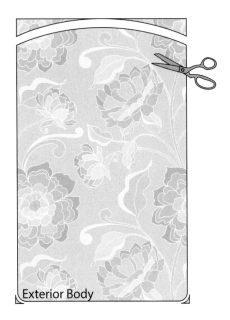

Figure 14

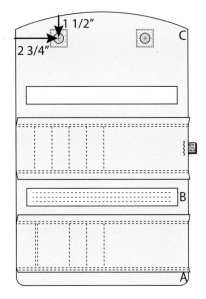

Figure 16

Sew-In Magnets

22 On the adhesive side of the Exterior Body Fusible Fleece piece, sew on the negative halves of the magnetic snap sets as shown. (Fig. 15) On the wrong side of the Interior, sew on the positive halves of the magnetic snap sets as shown. (Fig. 16)

Tip: For the fusible fleece, the magnetic attraction should be outward with the fusible fleece adhesive layer also facing outward. For the Interior, be sure the magnetic attraction is outward as the piece lays on the table with the right-side up. Don't be surprised when the magnets try to attract to your sewing machine.

23 According to the manufacturer's instructions, fuse the fusible fleece to the wrong side of the Exterior Body.

Tip: To give added integrity to the vinyl covering the magnets, place a 1½" (3.8cm) piece of cotton over the magnet so it is sandwiched between two pieces of cotton when topstitched in place.

Tip: Be careful not to press over the areas that have the magnet. Also, double-check that the fusible fleece doesn't stretch so the magnets are no longer in the correct position.

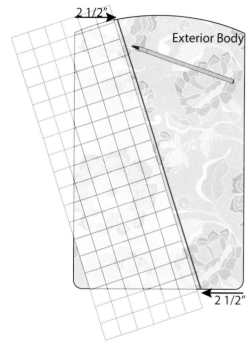

Figure 17

Ruffle, Optional

24 With the Exterior Body arched side up, draw a diagonal line beginning 2½" (6.5cm) in from the arched edge and ending 2½" (6.5cm) in, toward the other corner, from the straight edge. (Fig. 17)

25 Sew a pair of gathering stitches along the length of the RUFFLE ¼" (6mm) from each side of center.

26 Align the Ruffle wrong side to the Exterior Body right side. Pull the top threads of the Ruffle evenly to gather along the diagonal line. Topstitch down the center of the Ruffle twice.

not to clip through the stitching. (Fig. 18) Insert the Pocket piece through the slit to the wrong side of the Body and press around the opening, creating a finished window slot.

Zipper Pocket

27 Lay the ZIPPER POCKET over the Exterior Body, right sides facing, with the arched side up, as shown. (Fig. 18)

28 On the wrong side of the Pocket, draw a rectangle 7¼" × ⅝" (18.5cm × 1.5cm) as shown. (Fig. 18) Sew along the rectangle. Cut down center of the sewn rectangle and into each corner, being careful

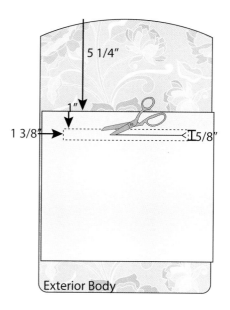

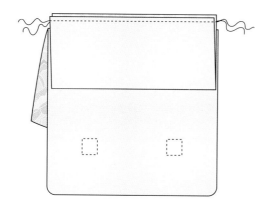

5 1/4"

1"

1 3/8"

5/8"

Exterior Body

Figure 18

Figure 20

29 Center the 7" (18cm) sport zipper on the inside of the Pocket through the opening with the zipper facing out. From the right side, topstitch at ⅛" (3mm). (Fig. 19)

30 Fold the Pocket fabric in half, right sides facing. Folding the Body out of the way, sew the top edge of the Pocket at ¼" (6mm). (Fig. 20) Pin the sides of the Pocket to the Body.

Body Assembling

31 Align the Exterior Body with the Interior, right sides facing. Tuck the Wrist Strap inside. Sew the perimeter with a ½" (1.3cm) seam allowance leaving a 6" (15cm) opening at the long center of Rectangle B for turning. (Fig. 21) See page 13 for hints on sewing and clipping curves.

32 Trim the seam allowance to ¼" (6mm) on the straight edges and ⅛" (3mm) on the curves. Do not trim the ends off the Wrist Strap. Turn right-side out.

> Tip: Be gentle with the insert pages. If you have pins holding the second Peltex piece in place, be careful not to let those come out or damage any of the clear vinyl as you turn right-side out.

Press flat being careful not to get heat on the clear vinyl.

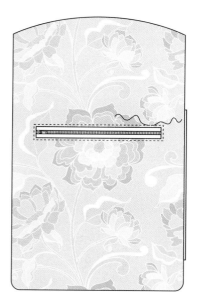

Figure 19

33 Tuck the END SUPPORT piece into the arch of the wallet through the opening in Rectangle B. (Fig. 21) Trim a little if it doesn't fit smoothly into place. It should be snug, but not buckling, and have about ⅛" (3mm) between it and the Peltex rectangle.

34 From the right side, topstitch four vertical lines next to each side of the interior Peltex pieces. (Fig. 22)

Tip: Feel through the layers to find the edges of the Peltex pieces. The topstitching lines will be roughly as shown (Fig. 22). Sometimes there tends to be a little fullness between the layers because quilting cotton has more give than laminated cotton. To mitigate this problem, begin and end the topstitching ¼" (6mm) from the edges. Be careful not to catch the Clear Vinyl Pages in the stitches. To help keep topstitching lines straight, put the edge of a piece of tape along the topstitching line as a guide.

35 Blindstitch the opening closed by hand. (Fig. 22)

Tip: Pull the Interior side a little tighter than the Exterior so it doesn't buckle when the wallet is closed. Experiment before sewing.

36 Remove the gathering stitches if you included a Ruffle.

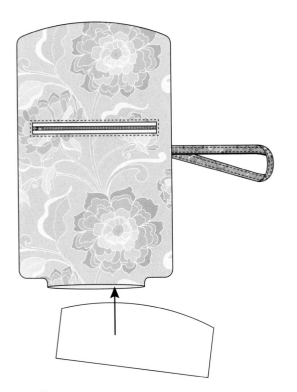

Figure 21

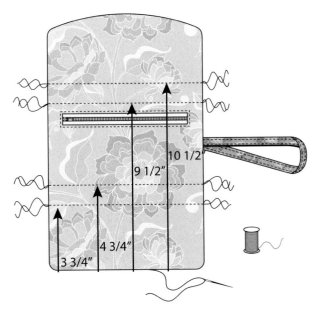

Figure 22

CHAPTER TWO

Totes and Bags

These totes and bags are anything but cliché. Absent are the stereotypical boxy designs. Each project offers unique function, while demonstrating style and fashion. The bags create a great canvas for accessorizing with a purpose and with a style that screams, "There is nothing ordinary about me!" The unique materials and variety of hardware might have you sewing out of your comfort zone, but don't be timid. I will lead you easily through the adventure.

Clear-as-Day Tote

This tote is for the confident woman. Show off your beach towels, shopping treasures, school projects, crafts or workout clothes. Don't try to hide anything here—actually, that isn't true. The *Clear-as-Day Tote* is transparent, but near the lower edges there are pockets to hide your keys or a wallet.

Size

14½" wide × 14" tall × 5" deep
(37cm × 35.5cm × 12.5cm)

Level of Difficulty (beginner)

Fabric Choices

Go crazy on this one with your choice of cotton for the accent. If you choose home décor weight fabric, omit the woven fusible interfacing. Heavy fabrics are not right for this pattern. Use 10- to 20-gauge clear vinyl. I've used 20-gauge for my tote. It is stiffer and more self-standing than 10-gauge, though it is a little trickier to work with.

Skills to Review

Cutting Bias Binding (page 15)
Sewing and Clipping Curves (page 14)
Sewing Laminated Cotton and Clear Vinyl (page 16)
Topstitching (page 14)
Working with Peltex (page 15)

Materials

Yardage

1½ yards (1.4m) exterior fabric (more if cutting on bias)

⅓ yard (30.5cm) clear vinyl

1¼ yards (1.1m) woven fusible interfacing, 20" (51cm) wide

18" × 10" (45.5cm × 25.5cm) piece of Peltex

18" × 20" (45.5cm × 51cm) piece of Soft and Stable

Notions

12" (30.5cm) elastic, ¼" (6mm) wide

Patterns

Clear-as-Day Tote patterns: Exterior Bottom, Peltex Bottom (on CD)

Featured fabric by Amanda Herring of The Quilted Fish

Cutting

> Note: Measurements are given as width × length. See cutting charts on the CD, if desired.

From exterior fabric, cut:

4 Rectangle C 15" × 5" (38cm × 12.5cm) for wide side of Lower Panel

4 Rectangle D 6" × 5" (15cm × 12.5cm) for narrow side of Lower Panel

2 Rectangle E 15" × 8" (38cm × 20.5cm) for wide side of Lower Pocket Panel

2 Rectangle F 10" × 8" (25.5cm × 20.5cm) for narrow side of Lower Pocket Panel

2 Bottom pieces from exterior pattern

2 rectangles 3½" × 29" (9cm × 73.5cm) for Handles

4 rectangles 2¼" × 3" (5.5cm × 7.5cm) for Handle Facings

4 rectangles 2¼" × 15½" (5.5cm × 39.5cm) Binding A

1 rectangle 3¼" × 42" (8.5cm × 106.5cm) for Binding B. This can be pieced and cut on bias.

1 rectangle 2¾" × 46" (7cm × 117cm) for Binding C. This is better if cut on the bias; it can be pieced.

From clear vinyl, cut:

2 Rectangle A 15" × 11" (38cm × 28cm) for wide side of Upper Panel

2 Rectangle B 6" × 11" (15cm × 28cm) for narrow side of Upper Panel

From woven fusible interfacing, cut:

2 rectangles 15" × 5" (38cm × 12.5cm) for wide side of Lower Panel

2 rectangles 6" × 5" (15cm × 12.5cm) for narrow side of Lower Panel

1 Bottom from exterior pattern

2 rectangles 3½" × 29" (9cm × 73.5cm) for Handles

From Peltex, cut;

2 Bottom pieces from Peltex pattern

From Soft and Stable, cut:

2 rectangles 15" × 5" (38cm × 12.5cm) for wide side of Lower Panel

2 rectangles 6" × 5" (15cm × 12.5cm) for narrow side of Lower Panel

1 Bottom from exterior pattern

Preparing the Pieces

1 According to manufacturer's instructions, fuse woven fusible interfacing to the wrong side of the Handles, two Rectangle C's, two Rectangle D's and one Bottom piece.

2 Pin Soft and Stable to the wrong side of the two Rectangles C to which you fused the interfacing, the two Rectangles D to which you fused the interfacing and one Bottom piece to which you fused the interfacing. Pull the fabric snug over the Soft and Stable.

3 Center both Peltex pieces to the wrong side of the other Bottom Piece. Topstitch around the Peltex at ⅛" (3mm).

Handles

4 Fold ½" (1.3cm) of all four sides of the HANDLE FACINGS, wrong sides facing, and press. (Fig. 1) Do this for all four Facings.

5 Fold ½" (1.3cm) of all four sides of one HANDLE, wrong sides facing, and press; then fold the Handle in half lengthwise. The finished width should be 1¼" (3.2cm). Topstitch the perimeter at ⅛" (3mm). (Fig. 2) All raw edges should be folded inside and hidden.

6 Position both ends of the Handle on RECTANGLE A in the positions illustrated. (Fig. 3) Pin only in the lower 2" (5cm) of the Handle.

7 Place a Handle Facing, wrong sides facing, at the lower end of the Handle with Rectangle A between them. From the exterior side, topstitch at ⅛" (3mm) around the perimeter of the Facing piece and through the end of the Handle, clear vinyl and Facing. Do this twice for added security. (Fig. 3) Repeat for the other end of the Handle and another Handle Facing.

8 Repeat the above steps to attach the other Handle to the other Rectangle A.

1/2"
1/2"

Figure 1

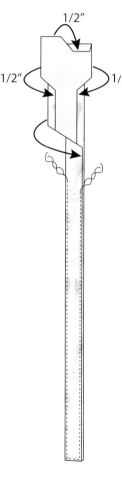

1/2"
1/2"
1/

Figure 2

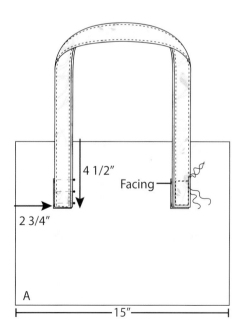

4 1/2"
Facing
2 3/4"
A
15"

Figure 3

Wide Side Lower Panels

9 Fold both RECTANGLE E's in half, bringing the long sides together, wrong sides facing. Topstitch the folded edge at ¼" (6mm). (Fig. 4)

10 Determine how many pocket divisions you desire. Fold Rectangle E's where divisions are to be and press, creating a line that will serve as a topstitching guide.

11 Set one Rectangle E on the right side of one RECTANGLE C without the Soft and Stable, aligning the lower and side raw edges. Baste the lower and side raw edges with a ¼" (6mm) seam allowance. Topstitch on both sides of the pressed lines that will divide the pocket sections. (Fig. 5)

12 Repeat for the other Rectangle E and the other Rectangle C without the Soft and Stable.

Narrow Side Lower Panels

13 Fold RECTANGLE F in half, bringing the long sides together, wrong sides facing. Topstitch the folded edge at ½" (1.3cm). This will become an elastic casing. (Fig. 6)

14 Sew a pair of gathering stitches along the bottom edge of Rectangle F. (Fig. 6)

15 Cut a 5½" (14cm) piece of elastic and fasten a safety pin to one end. Using the safety pin as a guide, thread the elastic through the casing. Baste the elastic ends in place at ¼" (6mm). (Fig. 7)

16 Set Rectangle F on the right side of one RECTANGLE D without the Soft and Stable, aligning the side raw edges with the top of Rectangle F 1" (2.5cm) down from the top of Rectangle D. The bottom corners of both panel pieces will match up.

By pulling the gathering stitches evenly, adjust the lower edge of Rectangle F to the same size as the lower raw edge of Rectangle D. Baste the bottom and side raw edges with a ¼" (6mm) seam allowance. (Fig. 7)

17 Repeat with the other Rectangle F and the other Rectangle D without the Soft and Stable.

Figure 4

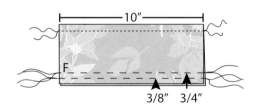

Figure 6

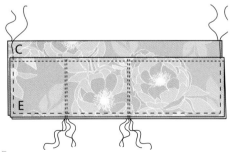

Figure 5

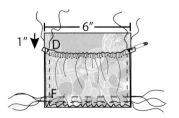

Figure 7

Assembling the Body

18 Align the top edge of one fabric Rectangle C (Pocket Panel from step 12) with one fabric RECTANGLE C EXTERIOR with the Soft and Stable, right sides facing. Insert one Rectangle A between the two Rectangle C's. Sew with a ½" (1.3cm) seam allowance. (Fig. 8) Trim off the Soft and Stable in the seam allowance.

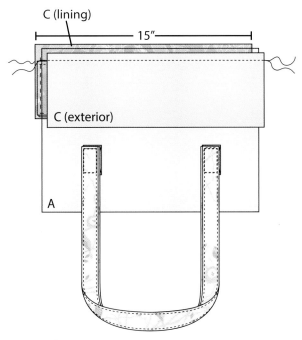

Figure 8

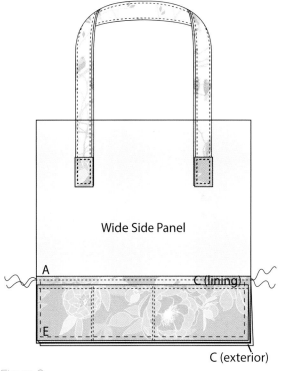

Figure 9

19 Turn right-side out so both Rectangle C's are wrong sides facing. Topstitch along the seam at ¼" (6mm). (Fig. 9)

20 Repeat for the other fabric Rectangle C's with vinyl Rectangle A. Use the same process to create side panels with fabric Rectangle D's and vinyl Rectangle B's. (Fig. 10)

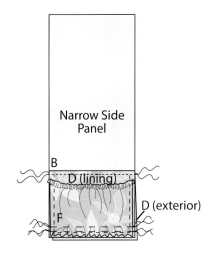

Figure 10

21 Fold the BINDING A's in half lengthwise, wrong sides facing, and press.

22 Align one Wide Side Panel with one Narrow Side Panel, lining sides facing. Align the raw edges of one Binding A piece with the raw edges of these two panels. Some Binding will overhang. Sew with a ½" (1.3cm) seam allowance with the Binding piece on top of the clear vinyl. This position is easier for the sewing machine to move over the clear vinyl. (Fig. 11)

23 Cut off the overhanging portion of the Binding. Trim the Soft and Stable in the seam allowance. Trim the seam allowance to ¼" (6mm). (Fig. 11)

24 Fold the rest of the Binding piece around the seam allowance extending ⅛" (3mm) beyond the previous stitching. Stitch in the ditch the length of the Binding. The result is a neatly covered seam. (Fig. 11)

25 Repeat until all four panels are sewn together and the seams are hidden.

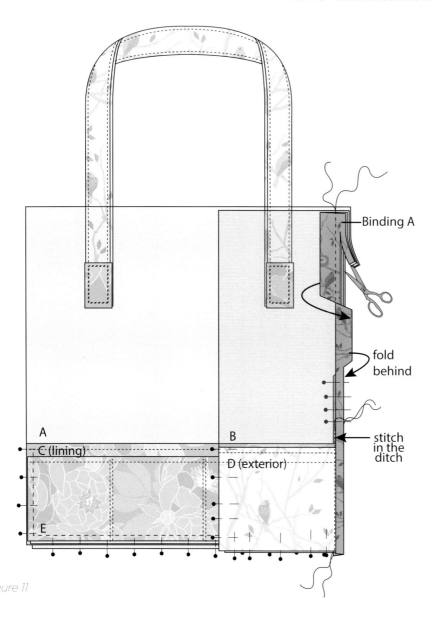

Figure 11

Bottom

26 Align both BOTTOM PIECES with each other, wrong sides facing. Baste the pieces together along the perimeter with a ½" (1.3cm) seam allowance. Trim the Soft and Stable to ⅛" (3mm). The side with Peltex will be the lining of the tote.

27 Cut ⅜" (1cm) clips through all layers along the lower raw edge of both Rectangle D's. Place the Body over the Bottom piece, lining sides facing. Align the Body center front and center back with the corresponding points on the Bottom. Use the clips in the fabric to allow for neat end curves.

Sew the perimeter with a ½" (1.3cm) seam allowance. (Fig. 12)

> Tip for all binding steps: There are many layers to sew in all the binding steps. Go slowly. This can only be sewn successfully from the top side of the tote. As you approach a curve, flatten the bottom out with the sides of the tote standing up. This will help the underside lay flat for stitching.

Remove the gathering stitches from the Rectangle F's. Trim the Soft and Stable in the seam allowance to ⅛" (3mm).

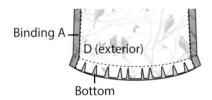

Figure 12

28 Fold the BIAS BINDING C in half lengthwise, wrong sides facing, and press. Open one end of the Binding and fold the raw end over ½" (1.3cm), wrong sides facing. Refold the Binding and press.

Place the folded end of the binding, right sides facing, at the center bottom of the exterior piece with the raw edges of the Binding even with the raw edge of the tote exterior. The binding is sewn to the side, not the bottom, of the tote.

Begin sewing the perimeter with a ½" (1.3cm) seam allowance 1" (2.5cm) from the folded end. (Fig. 13) Pull the Binding snug but don't stretch.

> Tip: Ease the Binding around the rounded edge. Make small clips in the Binding seam allowance to ease it smoothly.

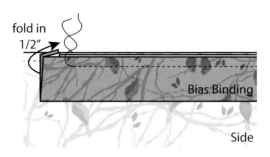

Figure 13

29 As the beginning fold approaches, gauge how much more Binding will be needed to finish, plus ½" (1.3cm) to tuck into the folded end. Trim off the excess. Tuck the raw end into the folded end. (Fig. 14) Continue sewing the Binding until the stitching overlaps the beginning stitching a little.

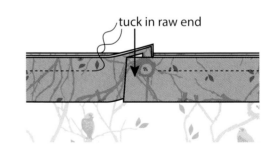

Figure 14

30 Trim the seam allowance to ¼" (6mm). Trim off any bulkiness.

31 Fold the rest of the Binding piece snugly around the seam allowance. It will extend slightly beyond the seam stitching. (Fig. 15) Stitch in the ditch. (Fig. 16)

Tip: There is a lot of thickness here. If needed, trim a little more of the seam allowance away so the Binding fits smoothly around. Also, double-check that the Binding is being caught on the underside during the stitching. The result should be a neatly covered seam. The hard part is over!

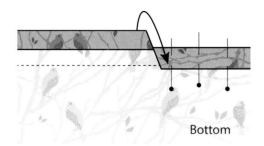

Figure 15

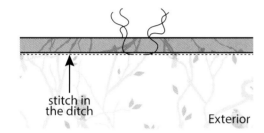

Figure 16

Top

32 Pin the Binding A's at the top toward the Narrow sides. Fold BINDING B in half lengthwise, wrong sides facing, and press. Open one end of the binding and fold in ½" (1.3cm). Refold the Binding and press.

33 From the inside, place the folded end of Binding B at the center of one of the big sides with the raw edges of the Binding even with the raw edges of the tote interior. Repeat steps 28, 29 and 31. Move the Handles out of the way while stitching. The result is a neatly covered seam.

Farmer's Market Tote

Who says you can't take it all? The *Farmer's Market Tote* is for the big shopping spree or an all-day outing. And while it's great for schlepping stuff, it also looks dressy and polished. The right fabric choices and fantastic size makes the bag feel like a win-win. The outside pocket is perfect for your phone and keys. The inside zipper pocket holds the other smaller necessities that can get lost in such a big bag. To sew a flimsy tote that can be stored in a suitcase or car for extra purchases, omit the fusible fleece.

Size
22" wide (at the top) × 12" tall × 7" deep
(56cm × 30.5cm × 18cm)

Level of Difficulty (easy)

Fabric Choices

Any cotton or home décor fabric will be perfect for the exterior. If a heavier fabric is chosen, it is recommended to keep the accent fabric and handles in cotton. Omit the fusible interfacing on pieces that have heavier fabric. The lining should be cotton.

Skills to Review

Installing a Magnetic Snap Set (exterior application)
   (page 18)
Topstitching (page 14)
Working with Peltex (page 15)

Materials

Yardage
⅔ yard (61cm) fabric for primary exterior

⅓ yard (30.5cm) fabric for secondary exterior

⅓ yard (30.5cm) fabric for accent (more if cutting on bias)

¾ yard (68.5cm) fabric for lining

¾ yard (68.5cm) fusible fleece

1¾ yards (1.6m) woven fusible interfacing, 20" (51cm) wide

14" × 25" (35.5cm × 63.5cm) piece of Peltex

Hardware
1 set of exterior magnets

4 metal center post buckles, 1" (2.5cm)

4 eyelet sets, ¼" (6mm)

Notions
1 sport zipper, 7" (18cm)

1 zipper, 7" (18cm)

1½ yards (1.4m) piping cord, ⁵⁄₃₂" (4mm)

Pattern
Farmer's Market Tote pattern: Zipper Pocket Plate (on CD)

Cutting

> Note: Measurements are given as width × length. See cutting charts on the CD, if desired.

From primary exterior fabric, cut:
2 rectangles 12" × 13" (30.5cm × 33cm) for Body
1 rectangle 16" × 8" (40.5cm × 20.5cm) for Bottom
2 rectangles 2¾" × 32" (7cm × 81.5cm) for Handles
1 rectangle 2¾" × 21" (7cm × 53.5cm) for Buckle Tab

From secondary exterior fabric, cut:
2 rectangles 12" × 13" (30.5cm × 33cm) for Body

From accent fabric, cut:
4 rectangles 1½" × 13" (3.8cm × 33cm) for Piping
1 rectangle 3¼" × 45" (8.5cm × 114.5cm) for Top Binding. Note: This can be pieced.
1 rectangle 11¼" × 4¾" (28.5cm × 12cm) for Zipper Pocket Plate

From lining fabric, cut:
1 rectangle 43" × 12½" (109cm × 31.5cm) for Body Lining
1 rectangle 15½" × 7½" (39.5cm × 19cm) for Bottom Lining
1 rectangle 12" × 13" (30.5cm × 33cm) for Zipper Pocket
1 rectangle 9¼" × 12" (23.5cm × 30.5cm) for Lining Pocket

From fusible fleece, cut:
4 rectangles 12" × 13" for Body
2 rectangles 1" × 31" (2.5cm × 79cm) for Handles

From woven fusible interfacing, cut:
4 rectangles 12" × 13" for Body
1 rectangle 16" × 8" (40.5cm × 20.5cm) for exterior Bottom
1 rectangle 2¾" × 22" (7cm × 56cm) for Buckle Tab

From Peltex, cut:
3 rectangles 14½" × 6½" (37cm × 16.5cm) for Bottom
1 Zipper Pocket Plate from pattern

Preparing the Pieces

1 According to the manufacturer's instructions, fuse woven fusible interfacing to the wrong side of the related pieces.

2 According to the manufacturer's instructions, fuse fusible fleece to the wrong side of the related Body pieces.

3 Center all three Peltex pieces to the wrong side of the exterior Bottom. Topstitch around the Peltex with a ⅛" (3mm) seam allowance.

Zipper Pocket

4 Lay one BODY PRIMARY EXTERIOR piece with the ZIPPER POCKET piece, right sides facing, with the 12" (30.5cm) sides up. Position the Pocket top edge 2¼" (5.5cm) down from the Body top edge. On the wrong side of the Pocket, draw a 7½" × ¾" (19cm × 2cm) rectangle as shown. (Fig. 1) Sew along the rectangle. Cut down the center of the sewn rectangle and into each corner, being careful not to clip the stitching. (Fig. 1) Insert the Pocket piece through the slit to the wrong side of the Exterior piece and press around the opening, creating a finished window slot.

5 Center the sport zipper to the inside of the Pocket through the opening with the zipper facing out. From the right side, topstitch at ⅛" (3mm). (Fig. 2)

Figure 2

Zipper Plate

6 Stretch the fabric ZIPPER POCKET PLATE over the PELTEX ZIPPER PLATE. Wrap the edges around to the back side of the Peltex and pin. On the back side, the curved areas will have a lot of overlapping fabric. For the piece to lay flat, trim away the excess fabric but not too close to the edge. Cut a line down the middle of the Zipper Plate fabric where the zipper opening is on the Peltex. Make small clips into each corner. Wrap those raw edges around to the back as well and pin. (Fig. 3)

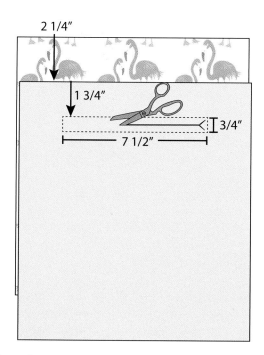

Figure 1

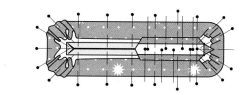

Figure 3

Tip: If you have fabric that might fray, I recommend making a small facing for the zipper opening. Cut a piece of cotton 9" × 2½" (22.9cm × 6.4cm). Center the Peltex Zipper Plate over the wrong side of the facing and trace the center rectangle opening onto the Facing. Remove the Peltex piece. Center the Facing over the Zipper Pocket Plate with right sides facing. Sew along the rectangle. Cut down the center of the sewn rectangle and into each corner, being careful not to clip the stitching. Turn right-side out through the opening. Press the edges square. Slip the Peltex piece between the fabric pieces keeping the seam allowance on the Facing side. Pull the fabric tight across the Peltex and pin all raw edges onto the back side as instructed in Step 6.

7 Center the opening of the Zipper Plate over the zipper from step 5. Topstitch the Plate through all layers at ⅛" (3mm) around the outer edge and the inner rectangle. (Fig. 4)

8 Fold the Zipper Pocket fabric in half, bringing the short ends together, right sides facing. Folding the Body out of the way, sew the top edge of the Zipper Pocket piece at ¼" (6mm). (Fig. 5) Pin the side raw edges of the Pocket and Body pieces together.

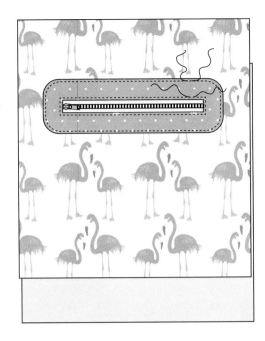

Figure 4

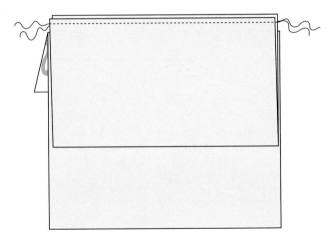

Figure 5

Piping

9 Cut the Piping Cord into four pieces 13" (33cm) long. Fold the PIPING fabric around the cord, wrong sides facing. With a piping or zipper foot, sew next to the cording with a seam allowance of about ½" (1.3cm), keeping the cord snug next to the foot. Repeat for all four Piping pieces. (Fig. 6)

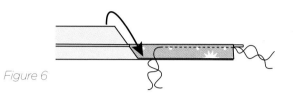

Figure 6

10 Align a 13" (33cm) side of one Body Primary Exterior with the raw edges of one Piping piece, right sides facing. Sew with a ½" (1.3cm) seam allowance using the stitching on the Piping as a guide. Align a 13" (33cm) side of one BODY SECONDARY EXTERIOR piece with this same Piping piece, right sides facing. Using the previous stitching as a guide, sew with a ½" (1.3cm) seam allowance.

Tip: When sewing next to the piping, use the zipper/piping foot.

Check that the new seam covers the stitching on the Piping. The result is that the two Body pieces are right sides facing with Piping between them. Fold the seam allowance toward the Primary fabric side and topstitch at ¼" (6mm).

11 Repeat for all four Body panels, alternating between primary and secondary exterior fabrics with a piece of piping between each panel. The piece becomes a loop. (Fig. 7)

12 Turn wrong-side out.

Bottom

13 Along the bottom edge of the Body, cut four ½" (1.3cm) clips 2" (2.5cm) from each Piping seam on the Secondary Fabric. There will be four clips. Position the Body over the BOTTOM piece, right sides facing. Center the Body front and back with the long edges of the Bottom. Spread the clips open to turn the Bottom corners. (Fig. 8) Sew the perimeter twice for added strength with a ½" (1.3cm) seam allowance. Turn right-side out.

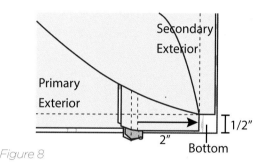

Figure 8

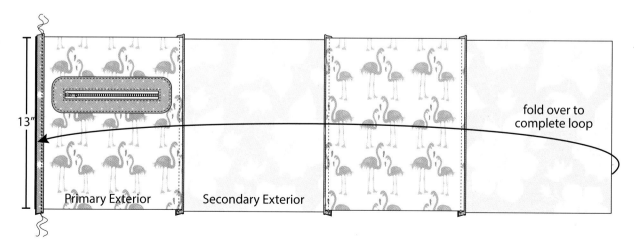

Figure 7

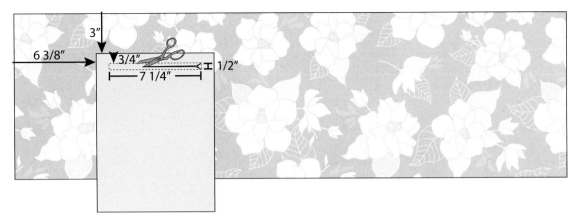

Figure 9

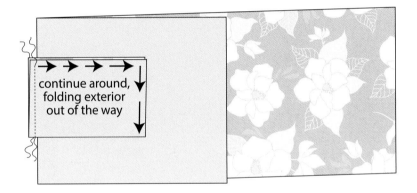

Figure 10

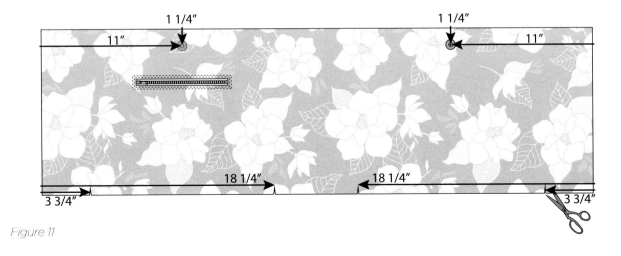

Figure 11

Lining Pocket

14 Place the LINING POCKET piece on top of the BODY LINING piece as shown, right sides facing, with 12" (30.5 cm) side of the Pocket positioned at the top and bottom. Draw a 7¼" × ½" (18.5cm × 1.3cm) rectangle as shown. (Fig. 9) Topstitch the rectangle. Cut down the center of the rectangle and out into each corner, being careful not to clip through the stitching. (Fig. 9) Insert the Pocket piece through the slit to the wrong side of the Lining and press around the opening, creating a finished window slot.

15 Center the regular zipper to the inside of the Pocket through the opening with the zipper facing out. From the right side, topstitch the rectangle at ⅛" (3mm) and again at ¼" (6mm), making sure to secure the zipper in place.

16 Fold the Pocket fabric in half, right sides facing. Folding the Body Lining out of the way, sew the three raw edges of the Pocket with a ¼" (6mm) seam allowance. (Fig 10)

Magnets

17 Attach the two halves of a magnetic snap to the right side of the Lining Body as shown; a negative one on one side, and a positive on the other side. (See page 18 for more on attaching magnets.) (Fig. 11)

Lining

18 Along the bottom raw edge of the Body Lining make four ½" (1.3cm) clips 3¾" (9.5cm) and 18¼" (46.5cm) from both short side edges. (Fig. 11) Bring the short sides together and sew a side seam with a ½" (1.3cm) seam allowance.

19 Position the Body Lining over the BOTTOM LINING piece, right sides facing. The Lining seam will be along one short end of the Bottom piece. Spread the clipped fabric open to turn the Bottom corners. Sew the perimeter with a ½" (1.3cm) seam allowance. Leave wrong-side out.

Assembling the Body

20 Align the side seam of the Lining with the side of the Body Exterior, wrong sides facing. The pocket in the Lining will be against the opposite side of the Exterior pocket. Easing slightly, pin along the top.

Top Binding

21 Fold the BINDING in half lengthwise, wrong sides facing, and press. Open one end and fold the raw end over ½" (1.3cm), wrong sides facing. Refold the Binding and press.

22 Place the folded end at the center back of the exterior piece, right sides facing, with the raw edges of the Binding even with the raw edges of tote exterior. Begin sewing the perimeter with a ½" (1.3cm) seam allowance 1" (2.5cm) from the folded end. (Fig. 12) Pull the Binding snug but don't stretch.

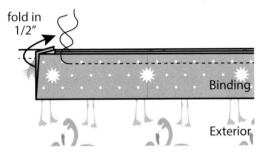

Figure 12

23 As the beginning fold approaches, gauge how much Binding will be needed to finish, plus ½" (1.3cm) to tuck into the folded end. Trim off the excess. Tuck the raw end into the folded end. (Fig. 13) Continue to sew the Binding until the stitching overlaps the beginning stitching a little.

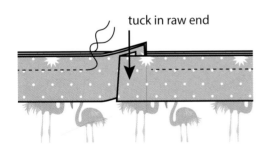

Figure 13

24 Fold the rest of the Binding piece snugly around the seam allowance. The fold will extend beyond the seam stitching about ⅛" (3mm). (Fig. 14) From the Exterior side, stitch in the ditch around the top. (Fig. 15)

Tip: If needed, trim a little of the Piping in the seam allowance away so the Binding fits smoothly around. Also, double-check that the Binding is being caught on the underside during the stitching. The result should be a neatly covered seam.

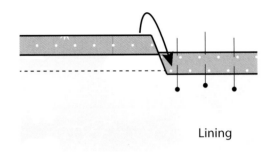

Figure 14

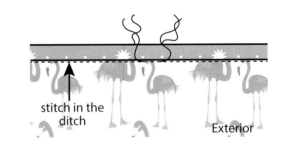

Figure 15

Buckle Tabs

25 Fold the lower raw edge up ¾" (2cm), wrong sides facing, and press. Fold the top raw edge over ⅜" (1cm), wrong sides facing, and press Fold the top folded edge over ⅝" (1.5cm), wrong sides facing and press. The finished width should be 1" (2.5cm). Topstitch down the center. (Fig. 16) Cut the Buckle Tab into four 5¼" (13.5cm) lengths.

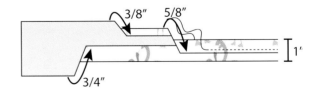

Figure 16

26 With each Buckle Tab, sew a ¼" (6mm) buttonhole centered 1¾" (4.5cm) in from the end. Thread the Tab through the buckle. Slide the catch of a buckle through the buttonhole and fold over the post 1¾" (4.5cm), seam to seam. Topstitch in place at ¼" (6mm). Fold the other end over ½" (1.3cm), seam to seam and pin. (Fig. 17)

Tip: Make sure that when the buckle faces outward, the catch is in the up position.

27 Position the Buckle Tab to the Primary Exterior Body at a slight angle as shown. (Fig 18) The buckle will face outward, and the folds are inward. All the raw edges should be hidden and the Lining lying flat underneath. Topstitch a rectangle ⅛" (3mm) away from the sides and bottom of the Tab and along the topstitching sewn in step 26. (Fig. 18) Repeat for added security. Repeat to attach all four Buckle Tabs to the bag.

Tip: To help the Lining not pucker, pin the lining from the inside to the fusible fleece in an area larger than the area that will be topstitched. Pull the Lining snug and flat. Be sure the pin ends will not interfere with the stitching from the other side. Then turn the bag over and pin the Tab to the exterior. Leave the pins in until you have finished topstitching.

Handles

28 Trim both lower corners of the Handle fusible fleece at a 45-degree angle.
According to the manufacturer's instructions, fuse the fusible fleece to the wrong side of one HANDLE as shown. (Fig. 19) Fold and press the length of the Handle as shown. Topstitch down the center. All edges should be folded inside and hidden. (Fig. 19)

29 Install an eyelet 9½" (24cm) from the center of the Handle. Install another eyelet toward the other end of the Handle at the same distance.

30 Repeat with the other Handle.

31 Thread the Handle ends through the buckles.

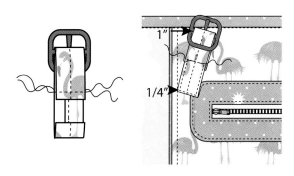

Figure 17   Figure 18

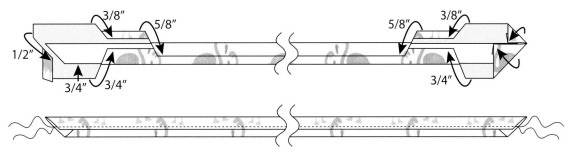

Figure 19

On-the-Go Bag

The free-spirited woman is on the go around town, along the boardwalk, climbing mountains (literal and figurative), schlepping kids and at the ball game. Hands-free convenience is essential for her. The *On-the-Go Bag* is the solution for this active woman. This bag features access through the top or zipper side opening, adjustable padded shoulder straps, a padded handle, a mobile phone pocket just inside the exterior zipper, a hanging key toggle, a drawstring closure at the top or O-ring hardware closing, and exterior pockets—all for convenience and style. Depending on your fabric choices, this backpack can be feminine or sporty.

Size

12" wide × 16½" tall × 6" deep
(30.5cm × 42cm × 15cm)

Level of Difficulty (experienced) ●●●●

Fabric Choices

The exterior fabric can be a heavyweight fabric such as laminated cotton, corduroy, twill or denim. If quilting cotton is chosen for the exterior, reinforce each piece with woven fusible interfacing. Quilting cotton is best for the lining. Refer to Repurposing Denim Jeans on page 15 for ideas on how to adopt denim ideas into this pattern. Denim is great on the bottom and patch pieces.

Skills to Review

Installing Purse Feet *(page 18)*
Repurposing Denim Jeans *(page 16)*
Sewing and Clipping Curves *(page 14)*
Topstitching *(page 14)*
Turning Narrow Pieces Right-Side Out *(page 15)*
Working with Peltex *(page 15)*

Featured fabric by Lila Tueller of Lila Tueller Designs

Materials

Yardage

1¼ yards (1.1m) fabric for exterior

1½ yards (1.4m) fabric for lining

⅓ yard (30.5cm) fabric for accent

¾ yard (68.5cm) fusible fleece

12" × 5½" (30.5cm × 14cm) piece of Peltex

16" × 9½" (40.5cm × 24cm) piece of Soft and Stable or fusible fleece

Hardware

1 metal swivel hook, 1¼" (3.2cm)

2 metal rectangles, 1¼" (3.2cm)

2 metal slides, 1¼" (3.2cm)

4 purse feet, 18mm, optional

1 metal swivel hook, ½" (1.3cm), optional for key toggle

Drawstring closure option: 1 metal D-ring, 1¼" (3.2cm)

O-ring closure option: 5 metal O-rings, 1¼ (3.2cm), and 1 metal rectangle, 1¼" (3.2cm)

Notions

2 sport zippers, 9" (23cm)

2 sport zippers, 7" (18cm)

Drawstring closure option: 1 drawstring toggle, optional

Pattern

On-the-Go Bag Template: Shoulder Strap Curve (on CD)

Cutting

> Note: Measurements are given as width × length. See cutting charts on the CD, if desired.

From exterior fabric, cut:
2 rectangles 17" × 19" (43cm × 48.5cm) for Front and Back Body

1 rectangle 11" × 4½" (28cm × 11.5cm) for upper piece of Short Outside Pocket

1 rectangle 11" × 8¾" (28cm × 22cm) for lower piece of Short Outside Pocket

1 rectangle 3½" × 16½" (9cm × 42cm) for left piece of Tall Outside Pocket

1 rectangle 5¼" × 16½" (13.5cm × 42cm) for right piece of Tall Outside Pocket

8 rectangles 1"* × 8½" (2.5cm × 21.5cm) for Zipper Strip. Note: Cut to width of zipper.

8 rectangles 3½" × 6" (9cm × 15cm) for Hardware Tabs

1 rectangle 5" × 24" (12.5cm × 61cm) for Hand Strap

2 rectangles 6½" × 16" (16.5cm × 40.5cm) for Padded Shoulder Strap

2 rectangles 3½" × 19" (9cm × 48.5cm) for Lower Shoulder Strap

From accent fabric, cut:
1 rectangle 16" × 9½" (40.5cm × 24cm) for Bottom

1 rectangle 8½" × 5" (21.5cm × 12.5cm) for Patch

1 rectangle 1½" × 44" (3.8cm × 112cm) for Drawstring, optional

From lining fabric, cut:
1 rectangle 11" × 4½" (28cm × 11.5cm) for upper piece of Short Outside Pocket

1 rectangle 11" × 8¾" (28cm × 22cm) for lower piece of Short Outside Pocket

1 rectangle 3½" × 16½" (9cm × 42cm) for left piece of Tall Outside Pocket

1 rectangle 5¼" × 16½" (13.5cm × 42cm) for right piece of Tall Outside Pocket

8 rectangles 1"* × 8½" (2.5cm × 21.5cm) for Zipper Strip. Note: Cut to width of zipper.

1 rectangle 19" × 16" (48.5cm × 38cm) for Side Interior Pocket

1 rectangle 35" × 18" (89cm × 45.5cm) for Lining

1 rectangle 9½" × 5½" (24cm × 14cm) for Lining Pocket

1 rectangle 2" × 9" (5cm × 23cm) for Key Toggle

From Peltex, cut:
1 rectangle 12" × 5½" for Bottom

From Soft and Stable, cut:
1 rectangle 16" × 9½" from Bottom

From fusible fleece, cut:
2 rectangles 17" × 16½" (43cm × 42cm) for Front and Back Body

4 rectangles 1"* × 8½" (2.5cm × 21.5cm) for Zipper Strip. Note: Cut to width of zipper.

2 rectangles 1¼" × 4" (3.2cm × 10cm) for Hand Strap

2 rectangles 6½" × 16" (16.5cm × 40.5cm) for Padded Shoulder Strap

Note
The illustrations show the Drawstring closure. Alternate instructions for the O-ring closure are in brackets.

Tip
If you're considering substituting Soft and Stable with fusible fleece for the body, remember that Soft and Stable will give more stability to the bag. However, the tricky steps of putting the sides on the body are awkward, and they're a little more difficult when using Soft and Stable. Fusible fleece is less firm, so it is easier to work with, but it will not hold up the sides of the bag independently.

Preparing the Pieces

1 If using quilting cotton for the exterior, fuse woven fusible interfacing to the wrong side of all related pieces, according to the manufacturer's instructions.

2 According to the manufacturer's instructions, fuse fusible fleece to the wrong side of all related pieces except the rectangles for the Hand Strap. For the Zipper Strips, fuse fusible fleece to four of the exterior Zipper Strip pieces. For the Body pieces, align and fuse fusible fleece to the bottom portions of the fabric pieces.

3 Baste Soft and Stable to the wrong side of the related Bottom piece with a ½" (1.3cm) seam allowance. Center Peltex to the Soft and Stable side of the Bottom piece and topstitch the perimeter of Peltex at ⅛" (3mm).

Zipper Strip Preparation

4 Align the short ends of one exterior ZIPPER STRIP piece with fusible fleece and one lining ZIPPER STRIP piece, right sides facing, with a 9" (23cm) zipper in the middle facing the exterior piece. Sew the short end with a ¾" (2cm) seam allowance.

(Fig. 1) Turn right-side out with the Zipper Strips wrong sides facing. Topstitch along the seam at ¼" (6mm). Repeat for the other end of the zipper with another set of exterior and lining Zipper Strip pieces. (See Zipper Strip in Fig. 2)

5 Repeat with the remaining three zippers. Use the exterior Zipper Strip pieces with fusible fleece with the 9" (23cm) zippers and the exterior Zipper Strip pieces without fusible fleece with the 7" (18cm) zippers.

Short Outside Pocket

6 Center one 7" (18cm) ZIPPER STRIP along the 11" (28cm) side of the exterior UPPER SHORT OUTSIDE POCKET piece with exterior fabrics right sides facing. Sew with a ¼" (6mm) seam allowance. (Fig. 2) Repeat with the other side of the Zipper Strip and the exterior LOWER SHORT OUTSIDE POCKET piece.

7 Trim off the overhanging portion of the Zipper Strip. Cut 1⅜" (3.5cm) squares out of all four corners of the exterior Short Pocket. (Fig. 3)

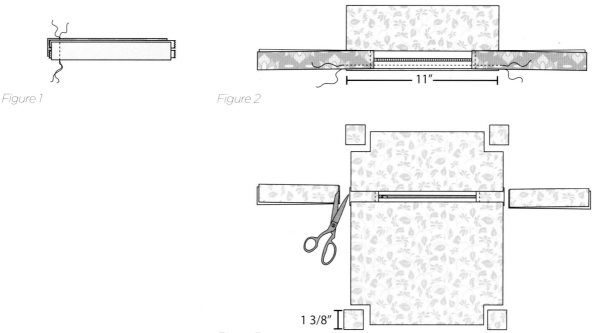

Figure 1

Figure 2

11"

Figure 3

1 3/8"

8 In each corner, fold the newly cut edges toward each other, right sides facing, and sew with a ½" (1.3cm) seam allowance. Do this for all four corners. Do the same with the LINING UPPER and LOWER SHORT OUTSIDE POCKET pieces in related corners. (Fig. 4)

9 Fold in the 11" (28cm) sides of the lining Upper and Lower Pocket pieces ¼" (6mm), wrong sides facing, and press. (Fig. 5)

Tall Outside Pocket

10 With the second 7" (18cm) Zipper Strip, measure 2" (5cm) up from the top of the zipper and cut straight across. (Fig. 6)

11 Align the Zipper Strip with the long side of the exterior TALL OUTSIDE LEFT POCKET piece with exterior fabrics, right sides facing. Sew with a ¼" (6mm) seam allowance. Repeat with the other side of the Zipper Strip and exterior TALL OUTSIDE RIGHT POCKET piece.

12 Trim off the overhanging portion of the Zipper Strip. Cut 2¼" (5.5cm) squares out of all four corners of the exterior Tall Pocket. (Fig. 7)

13 Fold in the newly cut edges toward each other, right sides facing, and sew with a ½" (1.3cm) seam allowance. Do this for all four corners. Do the same with the LINING RIGHT and LEFT TALL OUTSIDE POCKET pieces in related corners. (see Fig. 4)

14 Fold the 16½" (42cm) sides of the Lining Right and Left Pocket pieces ¼" (6mm), wrong sides facing, and press. (Fig. 5)

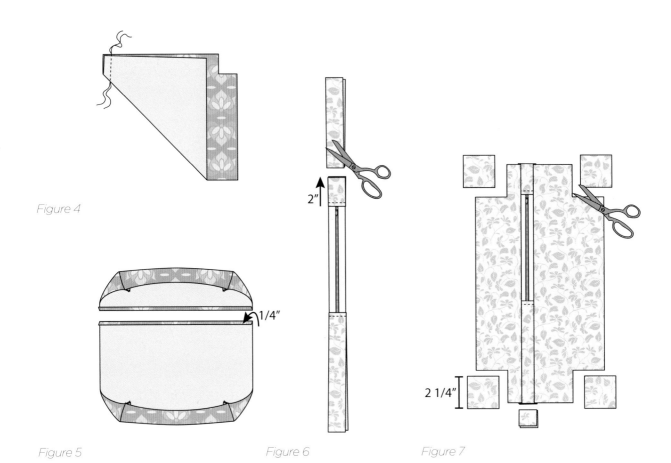

Figure 4

Figure 5

Figure 6

Figure 7

Finishing the Outside Pockets

15 For both Pockets, align the corresponding corners of the exterior and the lining Pocket pieces, right sides facing, and pin. Fold the seam allowance from the Zipper Strip away from the zipper. Sew the perimeter with a ½" (1.3cm) seam allowance. (Fig. 8) Turn right-side out.

16 Align the pressed edges of the lining Pocket pieces with the stitching along the Zipper Strip and pin. From the exterior side, topstitch along the zipper seams at ⅛" (3mm) and again ¼" (6mm). This will catch the pressed edges of the lining. (Fig. 9)

17 Pin the Short and Tall Pockets, lining sides down, to the right side of the BODY FRONT piece as illustrated. Topstitch the perimeter of each pocket at ⅛" (3mm). (Fig. 10)

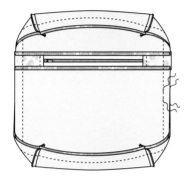

Figure 8

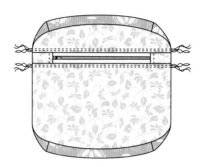

Figure 9

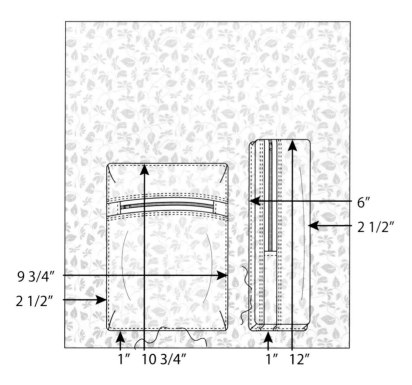

Figure 10

Lower Shoulder Strap

18 Fold over the edges of the LOWER SHOULDER STRAP, wrong sides facing, as illustrated and press. (Fig. 11) The finished width should be 1¼" (3.2cm). Topstitch down the center. (Fig. 11)

19 Thread the finished end around the center post of the metal slide and overlap, seam to seam, 1½" (3.8cm). Topstitch at ⅛" (3mm). Thread the raw end of the strap through the metal rectangle and then back through the slide, keeping seam against seam. (Fig. 12)

20 Repeat with the remaining Lower Strap and the remaining metal slide and metal rectangle.

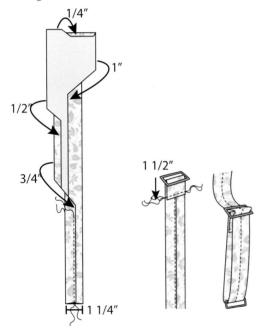

Figure 11   Figure 12

Padded Shoulder Strap

21 Bring the long sides of the PADDED SHOULDER STRAP together, right sides facing. Sew with a ½" (1.3cm) seam allowance. Maneuver the piece around so the seam is down the center. Using the template, cut a curved edge on one end. Sew the curve with a ¼" (6mm) seam allowance. Clip the corners and curve (page 14). Turn right-side out (see page 14 for tips on turning narrow pieces). Topstitch the perimeter at ⅛" (3mm) and again at ¼" (6mm). (Fig. 13)

22 Repeat with the remaining Padded Shoulder Strap.

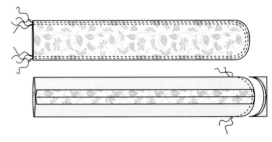

Figure 13

Hand Strap

23 Bring the long sides of the HAND STRAP together, right sides facing. Sew with a ½" (1.3cm) seam allowance. Turn right-side out. Maneuver the piece around so the seam is down the center.

24 Thread the Hand Strap through the 1¼" (3.2cm) swivel hook to the center and fold in half, seam to seam. Stack two fusible fleece rectangles between the two halves of the Hand Strap as illustrated. Topstitch a 5" × 1¾" (12.5cm × 4.5cm) rectangle around the fusible fleece as illustrated. The fusible fleece should now be hidden by topstitching. (Fig. 14)

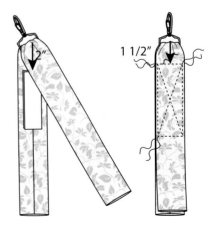

Figure 14

Patch

25 Cut away the lower corners of the PATCH as illustrated. (Fig. 15)

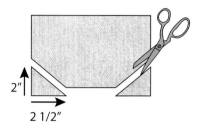

2"

2 1/2"

Figure 15

26 Align the two Padded Shoulder Straps (seam sides down) and the Hand Strap (in the center) to the right side of the Patch, with raw edges overhanging 1" (2.5cm). Baste with a ½" (1.3cm) seam allowance along the top edge of the Patch. (Fig. 16)

27 Turn the Patch over, so the wrong side is facing up, with the Straps/Handle extending away. Fold the raw edges of the Patch over, wrong sides facing, as illustrated and press. (Fig. 17)

Assembling the Back Body

28 Trim the raw edges of the Lower Straps at a 45-degree angle, in opposite directions. Align the Lower Straps, seam side down, to the side of the BACK BODY, right side, ¾" (2cm) up from the lower edge. Topstitch as illustrated. (Fig. 18)

29 With the wrong side of the Patch against the right side of the Back Body, center the Patch 4½" (11.5cm) down from the top. Pin the Patch in place with the three straps extending upward. Stitch in the ditch between the Patch and Straps. Topstitch the Patch perimeter at ⅛" (3mm) and again at ¼" (6mm). For added support, topstitch along the straight edge one more time at 1" (2.5cm). (Fig. 18)

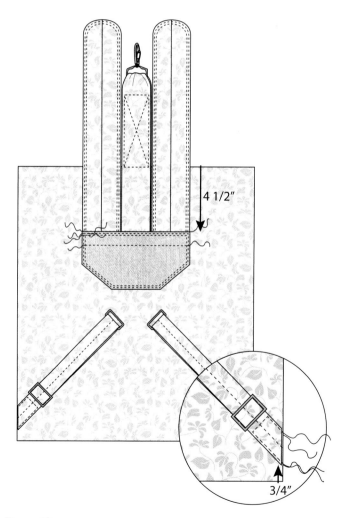

4 1/2"

3/4"

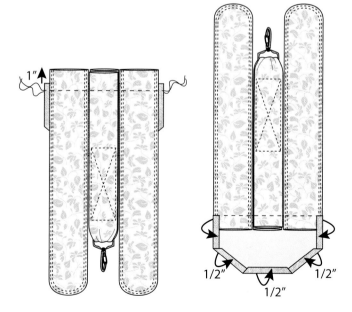

1"

1/2"   1/2"

1/2"

Figure 16   *Figure 17*   *Figure 18*

Side Interior Pocket and Zipper

30 Measure 7" (18cm) up from the top of the zipper on one 9" (23cm) ZIPPER STRIP and cut straight across. Pin the Zipper Strip along the left side of the Front Body, exterior sides facing. The lower end of the Zipper Strip will extend beyond the Front Body; trim the excess. Starting at the bottom of the Zipper Strip, align the 15" (38cm) side of the SIDE INTERIOR POCKET right side to the lining side of the Zipper Strip. Sew the full length of the Zipper Strip with a ¼" (6mm) seam allowance. (Fig. 19)

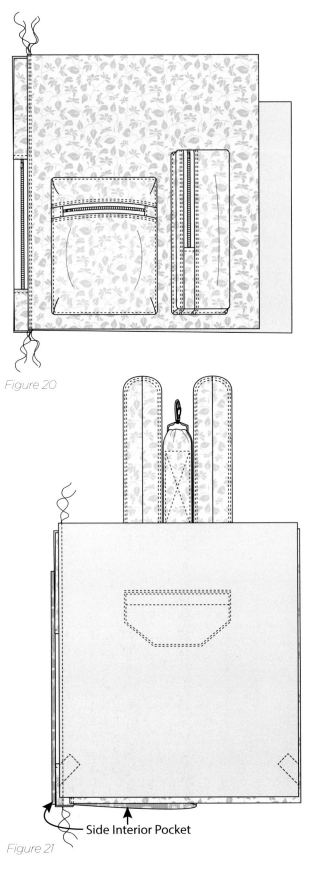

Figure 20

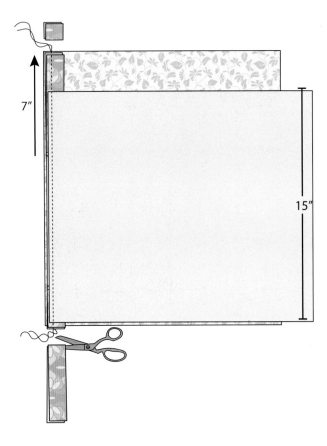

7"

15"

Figure 19

31 Open right-side out with the Pocket and Body wrong sides facing. Topstitch along the Zipper Strip at ⅛" (3mm) and again at ¼" (6mm). (Fig. 20)

Side Interior Pocket

Figure 21

32 Align the right side of the Back Body and the free side of the Side Interior Pocket to the left side of the Zipper Strip. The Side Interior Pocket will face the lining side of the Zipper Strip, and the Back Body will face the exterior side of the Zipper Strip. Sew with a ¼" (6mm) seam allowance. (Fig. 21)

Tip: Be sure to catch only the portion of the Side Interior Pocket that is adjacent to the seam in the topstitching; don't sew the pocket closed. This is a little tricky.

33 Open right-side out. Fold the Back Body and the Side Interior Pocket away from the Zipper Strip to prevent sewing the pocket closed. Topstitch at ⅛" (3mm) and again at ¼" (6mm).

34 Fold the Pocket toward the Back Body. Baste the lower portion of the Pocket in place with a ½" (1.3cm) seam allowance. Hand-baste the top portion of the Pocket in place with a ½" (1.3cm) seam allowance. (Fig. 22) You'll remove the hand-basting later.

Hardware Tabs

35 Fold the long sides of a HARDWARE TAB ½" (1.3cm), wrong sides facing, and press. Fold in half, wrong sides facing, and press. Topstitch both long sides at ⅛" (3mm) and again at ¼" (6mm). (Fig. 23) Repeat with all eight Hardware Tabs.

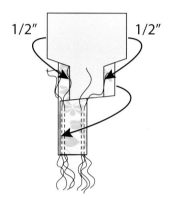

Figure 23

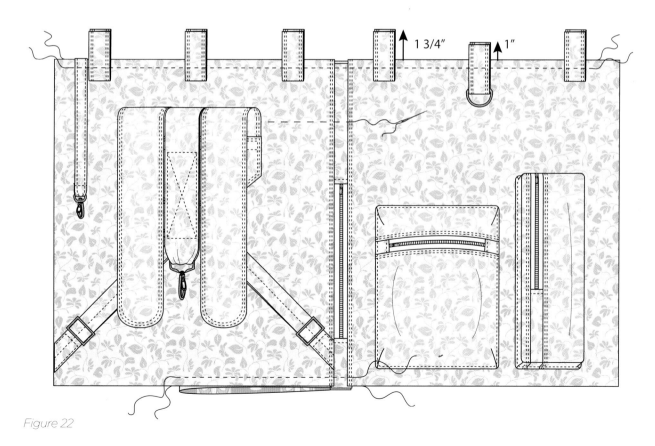

Figure 22

36 Thread one Tab through the D-ring [or metal rectangle for the O-ring closure] and fold in half, bringing the raw edges together. Fold five of the Tabs in half, bringing the raw edges together. [For the O-ring option, thread these five Hardware Tabs through five O-rings, and then fold in half.] Set aside the remaining two Hardware Tabs.

37 Pin the six folded Tabs along the top raw edge of the Exterior Body right side as illustrated. (Fig 22) Place the Tab with the D-ring [or metal rectangle] at the center of the Front Body, extending the raw edges of the Tab 1" (2.5cm) beyond the Exterior raw edge. Evenly distribute the other 5 Tabs, extending the raw edges of the Tabs 1¾" (3.8cm) [1" (2.5cm) for O-ring option] beyond the Exterior raw edge. Baste the Tabs in place with a ½" (1.3cm) seam allowance. (Fig. 22)

Key Toggle

38 Fold the KEY TOGGLE over, wrong sides facing, and press as illustrated. Topstitch both long sides at ⅛" (3mm). (Fig. 24)

39 Thread the finished end through the ½" (1.3cm) swivel hook, and fold over ¾" (2cm). Topstitch or machine whipstitch at ⅛" (3mm) to secure.

40 Align the raw edge of the Key Toggle to the top raw edge of the Exterior Body right side in a convenient location. Baste in place with a ½" (1.3cm) seam allowance. (Fig. 22)

Tip: Placing the Key Toggle near the side zipper opening makes it easily accessible from outside of the bag.

Side Zipper Opening

41 Measure 7" (18cm) up from the top of the zipper on the remaining 9" (23cm) Zipper Strip and cut straight across. Position the Zipper Strip along one 19" (48.5cm) side of the Exterior Body, exterior sides facing. Trim the excess portion at the bottom. Sew with a ¼" (6mm) seam allowance. (Fig. 25)

42 Align the other side of the Zipper Strip to the remaining 19" (48.5cm) side of the Exterior Body, exterior sides facing. Sew with a ¼" (6mm) seam allowance.

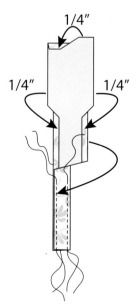

Figure 24

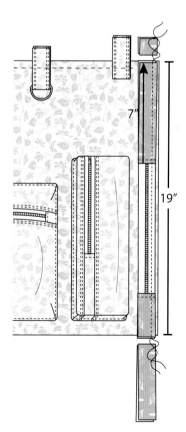

Figure 25

147

Bottom Piece

43 On the right side of the BOTTOM piece, mark 3½" (9cm) in from the short edges and 2¾" (7cm) in from the long edges on all four corners for purse feet placement.

44 Bring two adjacent sides of the Bottom together, right sides facing, forming a triangle at the corner. Sew a perpendicular line from the outer edge to the corner of the topstitching. Trim the excess corner fabric away to a ½" (1.3cm) seam allowance. (Fig. 26) Trim off the Soft and Stable in the seam allowance. Repeat with the other three corners. Turn right-side out.

45 Attach the purse feet (see instructions on page 18) at marked locations. (Fig. 26)

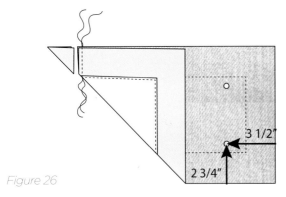

Figure 26

46 Align the lower edge of the Exterior Body to the Bottom, right sides facing, matching the front and back center points. Sew with a ½" (1.3cm) seam allowance. (Fig. 27)

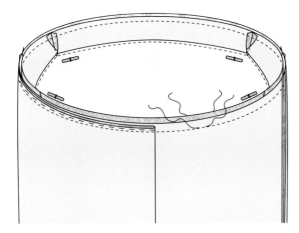

Figure 27

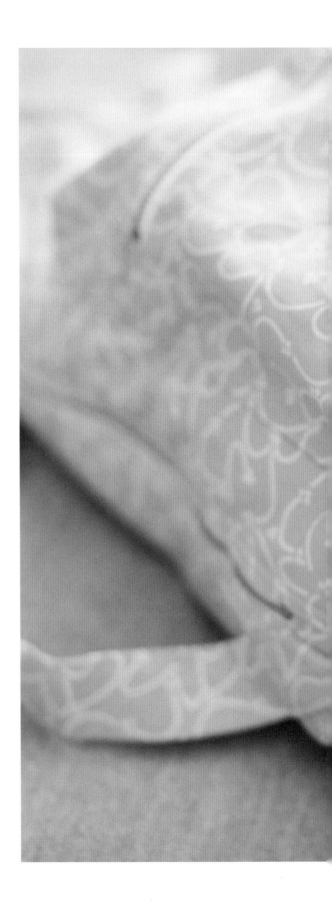

Lining

47 Fold the LINING POCKET in half, bringing the short sides together, right sides facing. Sew with a ¼" (6mm) seam allowance and press (be sure to use a pressing cloth if using laminate). Maneuver the pocket around so the seam is centered. Sew the top of the Pocket with a ¼" (6mm) seam allowance. Clip the corners. (Fig. 28) Turn right-side out. Topstitch the top at ¼" (6mm). To hide the raw edges, fold the lower edge in ¼" (6mm), wrong sides facing, and press. Position the Lining Pocket, seam side down, on the right side of the LINING piece 7½" (19cm) down from the top edge and 2" (5cm) in from the left side. Topstitch the Pocket sides and bottom to the Lining at ⅛" (3mm). (See stitching from wrong side in Figs. 29 and 30.)

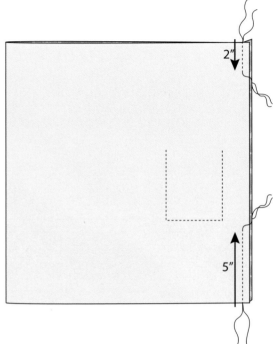

Figure 29

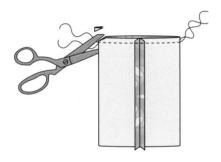

Figure 28

48 Fold the Lining in half, bringing the short sides together, right sides facing. Sew with a ½" (1.3cm) seam allowance as illustrated, leaving an 11" (28cm) opening. (Fig. 29) Press the seam open as if it were sewn all the way. Sew the bottom Lining edge with a ½" (1.3cm) seam allowance. (Fig. 30)

49 With right sides facing, maneuver the side seam so it is lined up with the bottom seam, forming a triangle. At a point 2½"– 3" (6cm–7.5cm) up from the corner, find the place where a 5" (12.5cm) line can be marked across the corner. (Fig. 31) Sew along the marked line. Repeat with the other side at the side fold (there is no side seam here).

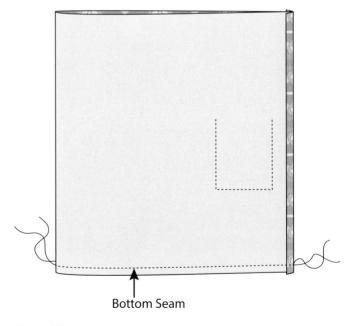

Bottom Seam

Figure 30

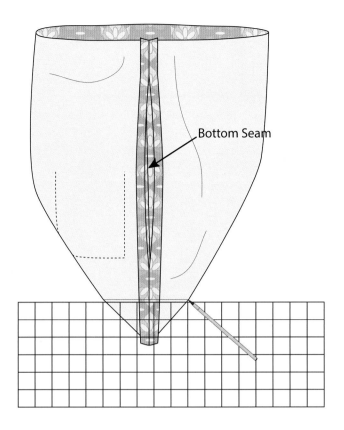

Bottom Seam

Figure 31

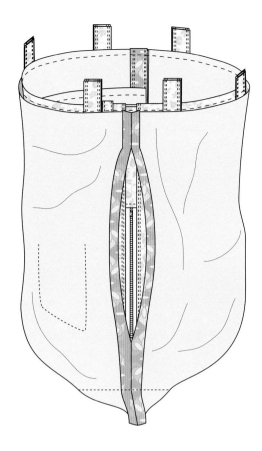

Figure 32

Assembling the Body

50 Tuck the Exterior Body inside the Lining, right sides facing. Align the side seam of the Lining with the Side Zipper Opening on the Exterior. (Fig. 32) Easing slightly, align the rest of the top raw edges with each other, right sides facing, and pin. Sew around the top raw edge with a ½" (1.3cm) seam allowance.

51 Turn right-side out through the Lining opening. Tuck the Lining inside the bag. Because the Lining is shorter than the Exterior, the Exterior Body will fold 2" (5cm) into the inside of the bag when turned right-side out. Pin the seam allowance and overhang from the Tabs in the down position. The hand basting on the Side Interior Pocket will keep the top of it tucked about 2" (5cm) into the fold. The

stitching will catch the top of the Pocket. Stitch in the ditch around the bag along the Exterior Body to the Lining seam. On the Back Body, the stitching in the ditch will line up with the top of the Patch. For added support, topstitch ¼" (6mm) down from the stitching in the ditch. (Fig. 33)

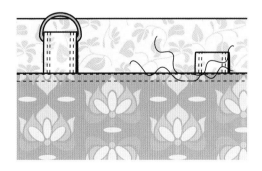

Figure 33

Drawstring Closure

Skip if using the O-ring closure.

52 Between the two Tabs above the Short Outside Pocket, sew two ½" (1.3cm) buttonholes ½" (1.3cm) apart and ¼" (6mm) above the stitching in the ditch. (Fig. 34)

53 Fold the DRAWSTRING, wrong sides facing, as illustrated and press. Topstitch at ⅛" (3mm). (Fig. 35)

Tip: For heavier fabric, cut the piece a little wider if these ¼" (6mm) folds are too small. Be creative!

54 Thread one end of the Drawstring through one buttonhole from the outside. Thread it through all six tabs and then out the other buttonhole. Cinch it tight and tie a bow or thread it through a drawstring toggle. Clip the large swivel hook onto the D-ring to secure the top Handle Strap.

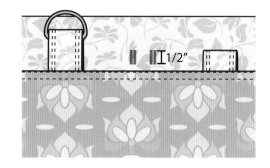

Figure 34

Tip: If you plan to use a drawstring toggle, omit the ½" (1.3cm) fold at the ends of the Drawstring. Once you thread the ends through the toggle in step 52, tie a little knot at the ends of the Drawstring to prevent fraying.

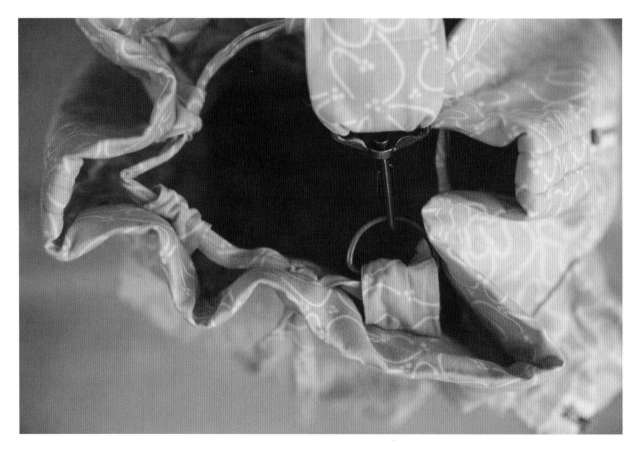

Figure 35

O-Ring Closure

Skip if using the Drawstring closure.

55 Turn the metal rectangle on the Tab so the short end is up; there will be fullness in the Tab at the bottom of rectangle. Thread the rectangle through all the O-rings and clip the large swivel hook to the rectangle. The bag is securely closed, and the Handle Strap can now be used.

Finishing

56 Remove the hand-basting that was holding the top portion of the Side Interior Pocket.

57 Evenly align the Lining opening that was pressed under ½" (1.3cm) to the stitching on the lining side of the Zipper Strip (Side Zipper Opening). From the exterior side, topstitch a rectangle around the zipper at ⅛" (3mm) and again at ¼" (6mm). (Fig. 36) Check that the opening in the Lining is completely closed.

58 Trim the two remaining Hardware Tabs to 4" (10cm). Thread one through the metal rectangle at the end of the right Lower Strap and fold, leaving one raw edge ¾" (2cm) longer than the other. Fold down the overhanging ¾" (2cm). (Fig. 37) Pin the Tab, raw edges down, to the right Padded Shoulder Strap, 3" (7.5cm) up from the curved edge and centered. Topstitch the folded-over portion of the Tab to the Padded Shoulder Strap as illustrated, hiding all raw edges. (Fig. 38) Repeat with the remaining Tab on the left Padded Shoulder Strap and left Lower Strap.

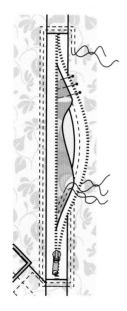

Figure 36

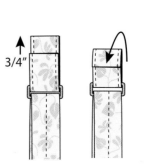

Figure 37

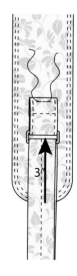

Figure 38

Province Travel Bag

The *Province Travel Bag* takes traveling in fashion to a creative level. Hang your ID or a couple of charms on the hangers. This bag features a removable shoulder strap, over-the-arm handles, an easy-to-get-to mobile phone pocket in the front with a flap, two exterior side pockets with magnetic snaps for security and a top zipper to keep everything securely stored. Multiple interior pockets help keep everything organized. With the right fabric choices, this bag will help you express your inner funk.

Size

20" wide × 16" tall × 10½" deep
(51cm × 40.5cm × 26.5cm)

Level of Difficulty (easy)

Fabric Choices

This pattern is designed for quilting cotton. If home décor or heavier fabric is chosen, leave off the woven fusible interfacing. Home décor fabric could work for the lining, but that will make the seam allowance pretty thick and a little tricky to cover with binding. Cotton is easiest for the lining. There are several possibilities for a variety of accent fabrics, so go creative if you're in the mood.

Skills to Review

Installing a Magnetic Snap Set (exterior application) (page 18)
Installing Purse Feet (page 18)
Sewing and Clipping Curves (page 14)
Turning Narrow Pieces Right Side Out (page 15)
Working with Peltex (page 15)

Featured fabric by Amanda Herring of The Quilted Fish

Materials

Yardage

1⅓ yards (1.2m) fabric for exterior

2 yards (1.8m) fabric for lining

1 yard (91.5cm) fabric for accent

3½ yards (3.2m) woven fusible interfacing, 20" (51cm) wide

1 yard (91.5cm) fusible fleece

18" × 23" (45.5cm × 58.5cm) piece of Peltex

12" × 36" (30.5cm × 91.5cm) piece of Soft and Stable

Hardware

2 sets of exterior magnets

2 D-rings, 1¼" (3.2cm)

4 metal rectangles, 1¼" (3.2cm)

2 swivel hooks, 1¼" (3.2cm)

6 purse feet, 18mm

2 swivel hooks, ½" (1.3cm), optional

Notions

1 sport zipper, 22" (56cm)

1 zipper, 12" (30.5cm)

3 yards (2.7m) of bias tape extra-wide double-fold, ½" (1.3cm)

Patterns

Province Bag patterns: Front Pocket Flap, Side (on CD)

Cutting

> Note: Measurements are given as width × length. See cutting charts on the CD, if desired. Alternate cutting instructions for wider straps are also included in the cutting chart on the CD.

From exterior fabric, cut:

2 rectangles 20" × 22¼" (51cm × 56.5cm) for Body
2 Side pieces from pattern
2 Rectangle A 12½" × 8" (31.5cm × 20.5cm) for Side Pocket
2 Front Pocket Flap pieces from pattern

From lining fabric, cut:

2 rectangles 20" × 23¾" (51cm × 60.5cm) for Body
2 Side pieces from pattern
2 Rectangle C 11¼" × 17" (28.5cm × 43cm) for Lining Side Pockets
1 Rectangle F 10" × 14" (25.5cm × 35.5cm) for Front Pocket
1 Rectangle G 14" × 24" (35.5cm × 61cm) for Lining Zipper Pocket
1 Rectangle H 11" × 11" (28cm × 28cm) for Lining Small Pocket

From accent fabric, cut:

2 Rectangle B 12½ × 10" (31.5cm × 25.5cm) for Side Pocket
1 Rectangle D 2½" × 7½" (6.5cm × 19cm) for Zipper and Front Pocket Pull Tab
1 Rectangle E 3½" × 9" (9cm × 23cm) for D-Ring Tabs
2 rectangles 47" × 2¾" (119.5cm × 7cm) for Handle Straps. These can be pieced.
1 rectangle 2" × 20" (5cm × 51cm) for Charm Hanger, optional
2 Rectangle J 20" × 2½" (51cm × 6.5cm) for Zipper Strips
2 rectangles 3½" × 24" (9cm × 61cm) for Handles
1 rectangle 3½" × 38" (9cm × 96.5cm) for Shoulder Strap

From woven fusible interfacing, cut:

2 rectangles 20" × 22¼" (51cm × 56.5cm) for Body
2 Side pieces from pattern
2 Rectangle A 12½" × 8" (31.5cm × 20.5cm) for Side Pocket

2 Rectangle B 12½" × 10" (31.5cm × 25.5cm) for Side Pocket
1 Rectangle E 3½"x 9" (9cm × 23cm) for D-Ring Tabs
2 Front Pocket Flap pieces from pattern
2 rectangles 47" × 2¾" (119.5cm × 7cm) for Handle Straps. These can be pieced.
2 Rectangle J 20" × 2½" (51cm × 6.5cm) for Zipper Strips

From fusible fleece, cut:

2 rectangles 20" × 22¼" (51cm × 56.5cm) for Body
2 Rectangle J 20" × 2½" (51cm × 6.5cm) for Zipper Strips
2 rectangles 1¼" × 23" (3.2cm × 58.5cm) for Handles
1 rectangle 1¼" × 37" (3.2cm × 94cm) for Shoulder Strap

From Peltex, cut:

3 rectangles 18" × 7½" (45.5cm × 19cm) for Bottom

From Soft and Stable, cut:

2 Side pieces from pattern

> **Tip**
>
> If you're considering substituting Soft and Stable with fusible fleece for the body, remember that Soft and Stable will give more stability to the bag. However, the tricky steps of putting the sides on the body are awkward, and they're a little more difficult when using Soft and Stable. Fusible fleece is less firm, so it is easier to work with, but it will not hold the sides of the bag up independently.

Preparing the Pieces

1 According to the manufacturer's instructions, fuse woven fusible interfacing to the wrong side of the Body Exterior pieces, Side Exterior pieces, Handle Straps, Front Pocket Flap, and Rectangles A, B, E, and J.

2 According to manufacturer's instructions, fuse fusible fleece to the wrong side of the Body Exterior pieces and Rectangle J's.

Exterior Side Pocket

3 Align one each of RECTANGLES A and B along their long edges, right sides facing. Sew with a ½" (1.3cm) seam allowance. Press the seam allowance toward Rectangle B. Bring the long edges of the two pieces together, wrong sides facing. Even out so Rectangle B is 1" (2.5cm) onto the Rectangle A side. Press. (Fig. 1)

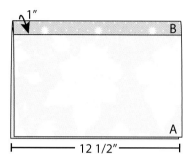

Figure 1

4 Make a mark on the Rectangle B side centered and ¾" (2cm) down from the fold. Open the piece. On the right side, install one half of a magnetic snap on that mark. Refold the pocket. (Fig 2)

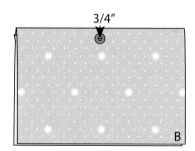

Figure 2

5 Align the folded edge of the Pocket with the SIDE EXTERIOR right side along the line indicated on the pattern with the magnet facing the Side Exterior. Using the magnet on the Pocket, locate the point where the other half of the magnetic snap should be on the Side Exterior. Install the magnet at this point. (Fig. 3) Reposition the Pocket over the Side. Double-check the location of the magnets.

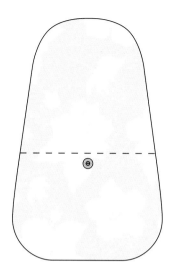

Figure 3

6 Turn the piece over with the wrong side up. Using the edge of the Side as a guide, baste the Pocket in place with a ½" (6mm) seam allowance. Trim the Pocket to match the Side shape. (Fig. 4)

7 Repeat for the other Rectangles A and B and the remaining Side Exterior piece.

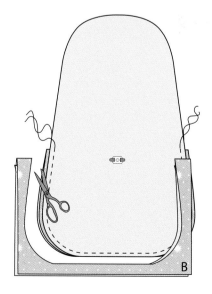

Figure 4

Lining the Side Pocket

8 Fold one RECTANGLE C in half, bringing the 11¼" (28.5cm) ends together, wrong sides facing. Top-stitch the fold at ¼" (6mm). (Fig. 5) Fold the Pocket where you choose to have divisions and press to create a pressed line as a sewing guide.

9 Place the Pocket on the SIDE LINING piece right side along the line indicated on the pattern piece.

10 Turn the piece over with the wrong side up. Using the edge of the lining piece as a guide, baste the Pocket in place with a ½" (6mm) seam allowance. From the right side, topstitch on both sides of the pressed line from step 8. (Fig. 6) Trim the Pocket to match the Side Lining shape.

11 Repeat for the other Rectangle C and remaining Side Lining piece.

12 Align both Side Exterior and Side Lining pieces, wrong sides facing, with Soft and Stable between them. (Fig. 7) Pull the fabric a little snug across the Soft and Stable and pin.

> Tip: If substituting with fusible fleece, fuse that now to the wrong side of the Side Exterior.

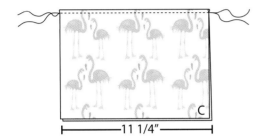

Figure 5

Figure 6

Figure 7

Zipper and Front Pocket Pull Tab

13 Fold RECTANGLE D in half with long sides together, right sides facing, and sew with a ¼" (6mm) seam allowance. (Fig. 8) Turn right-side out.

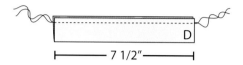

Tip: This is a perfect place to use the safety pin technique. See page 15.

Figure 8

14 Move the seam around so it is centered. Press flat. Cut into three 2½" (6.5cm) pieces. Fold all pieces in half, seam to seam, and press again.

15 Center a folded Tab at the top of both the right side Side Exterior pieces, matching raw edges. Sew at ½" (6mm) several times for added reinforcement (see Fig. 11).

16 Set aside the third Tab until step 22.

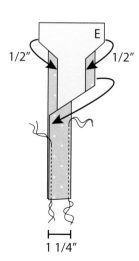

Figure 9

D-Ring Tabs

17 Fold both 9" (23cm) sides of RECTANGLE E over ½" (1.3cm), wrong sides facing, and press. Fold in half, wrong sides facing, and press. The finished width should be 1¼" (3.2cm). Sew both edges at ⅛"(3mm). (Fig. 9) Cut into two 4½" (11.5cm) pieces.

18 Slide one Tab through a D-ring. Fold the Tab as shown. (Fig. 10) Position on the Side Exterior piece and topstitch as illustrated. (Fig. 11) The raw edges of the Tab should all be hidden against the right side of the Side. Sew a 1" (2.5cm) square several times for added reinforcement.

19 Repeat for the other Tab and other Side Exterior.

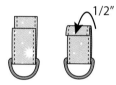

Figure 10

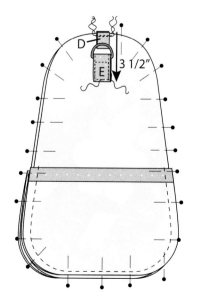

Figure 11

Front Pocket

20 Lay RECTANGLE F over one BODY EXTE-RIOR, right sides facing, with short sides up. Center the Pocket and place it 8" (20.5cm) down from the top edge of the Body. On the wrong side of the Pocket, draw an 8 × ½" (20.5cm × 1.3cm) rectangle as shown. (Fig. 12) Topstitch this drawn rectangle. Cut down the center of the sewn rectangle and into each corner, being careful not to clip through the stitching. (Fig. 12) Insert the Pocket piece through the slit to the wrong side of the Body and press around the opening, creating a finished window slot. Topstitch around the rectangle at ⅛" (3mm). (Fig. 13)

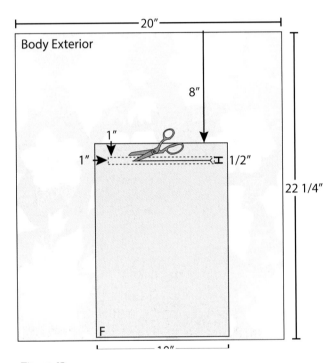

Figure 12

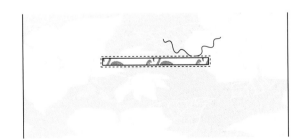

Figure 13

21 Fold the Pocket fabric in half, right sides facing. Pin the sides and top raw edges together. (Fig. 14)

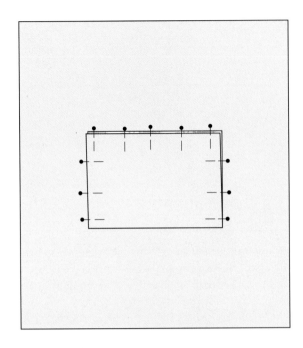

Figure 14

Front Pocket Flap

22 Center the raw edge of the Tab from step 16 along the FRONT POCKET FLAP curve on the right side. Align the two Front Pocket Flap pieces, right sides facing. Sew the curved edge with a ¼" (6mm) seam allowance. (Fig. 15) Trim the seam allowance (see page 14, Sewing and Clipping Curves) to ⅛" (3mm), but do not trim the raw edges of the Tab. Press the straight edges over ½" (1.3cm), wrong sides facing. Turn right-side out and press. Pin the straight edge together. (Fig. 16)

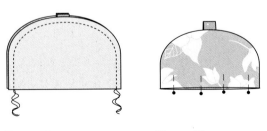

Figure 15   Figure 16

23 Center the pressed straight edges of the Flap above the top of the Front Pocket, right sides facing. Topstitch along the Flap straight edge at ⅛" (3mm) and again at ¼" (1.3cm). (Fig. 17)

Tip: When topstitching, be careful of pins holding the top of the Pocket in place. This topstitching will secure the Flap in place as well as sew the top of the Pocket together. All the raw edges of the Flap are hidden. Don't worry that the pocket opening is longer than the Flap; the ends of the Pocket opening will be covered by Handle Straps.

Figure 17

24 Fold the Flap down and press. Remove the pins holding the top of the Pocket in place.

Handle Straps

25 Sew the bottom seam of the Body Exterior by aligning the 20" (51cm) ends of the two pieces, right sides facing, and sew with a ½" (1.3cm) seam allowance.

26 Fold over both long sides of the HANDLE STRAP ¾" (2cm), wrong sides facing, and press; the sides will overlap each other. The finished width should be 1¼" (3.2cm). (Fig. 18)

27 Thread the Strap through a metal rectangle and fold the end over 2½" (6.5cm), wrong sides facing. Hide all raw edges. Topstitch across the Strap ½" (1.3cm) from the metal rectangle. (Fig. 19) Repeat with the other end of the Strap.

28 Repeat steps 26 and 27 with the remaining Handle Strap. If needed, adjust the Straps so they are exactly the same length.

Tip: When turning these corners, leave the sewing machine needle in the down position to rotate without losing the location of the corner. This topstitching hides the ends of the Pocket opening as well as secures the sides of the Front Pocket, so remove those pins now. This is the last chance you have to press the body flat.

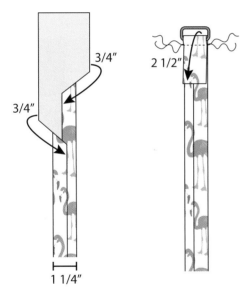

3/4"

3/4"

2 1/2"

1 1/4"

Figure 18

Figure 19

29 Align the Straps wrong side to the Body right side, as shown. (Fig. 20) The center of the Strap will match up with the bottom seam of the Body. Topstitch along both sides of each Strap at ⅛" (3mm). At the ends, toward the metal rectangles, turn to topstitch across the Strap 1½" (3.8cm) from the metal rectangle.

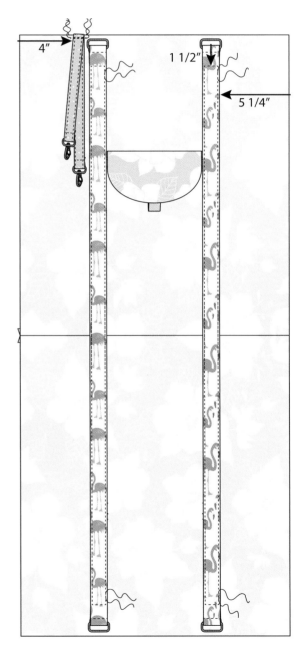

4"

1 1/2"

5 1/4"

Figure 20

Charm Hanger, Optional

30 Fold the CHARM HANGER, wrong sides facing, and press as illustrated. (Fig. 21) The finished width should be ½" (1.3cm). Topstitch both sides at ⅛" (3mm), hiding all raw edges.

31 Thread the Hanger through one ½" (1.3cm) swivel hook, overlapping ½" (1.3cm). Machine whipstitch in place hiding all raw edges. Repeat for the other swivel hook on the other end of the Hanger. Fold the Hanger, leaving one side longer than the other. Put that fold at the top raw edge of the Front Body right side 4" (10cm) in from the left side. Baste in place with a ¼" (6mm) seam allowance. (Fig. 20)

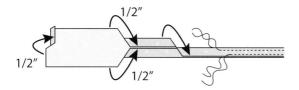

Figure 21

Bottom

32 Stack three Peltex pieces together. Center this stack to the wrong side of the Body Exterior. Topstitch the perimeter of the Peltex at ⅛" (3mm).

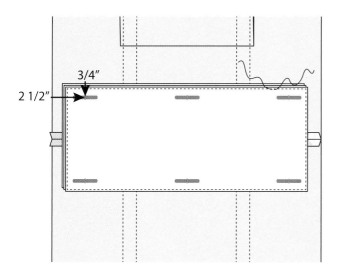

Figure 22

33 From the right side of the Exterior, attach the purse feet through the Peltex (page 18) as shown. (Fig. 22) There are a total of six.

> Tip: The purse feet will not completely protect the bottom of your bag, so be careful where you set it down.

Lining Zipper Pocket

34 Align RECTANGLE G and one BODY LINING piece right sides facing with short sides up. Center the Pocket and place it 4½" (11.5cm) down from the top of the Lining. Draw a 12¼" × ½" (31cm × 1.3cm) rectangle on the wrong side of the Pocket as shown. (Fig. 23) Topstitch this rectangle. Cut down the center of the sewn rectangle and into each corner, being careful not to clip through the stitching. (Fig. 23) Insert the Pocket piece through the slit to the wrong side of the Lining and press around the opening, creating a finished window slot.

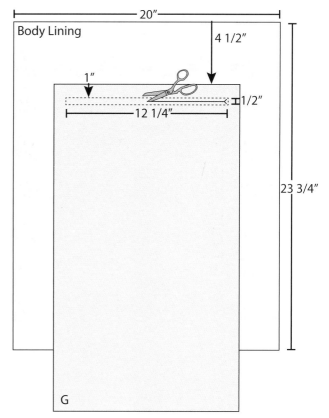

Figure 23

35 Center the 12" (30.5cm) zipper in this opening. From the right side of the Lining, topstitch at ⅛" (3mm) and again at ¼" (6mm). (Fig. 24)

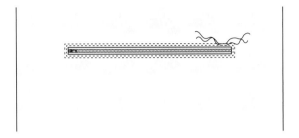

Figure 24

36 Fold the Pocket fabric in half, right sides facing. Moving the Lining out of the way, sew the three raw edges of the Pocket with a ½" (1.3cm) seam allowance. (Fig. 25)

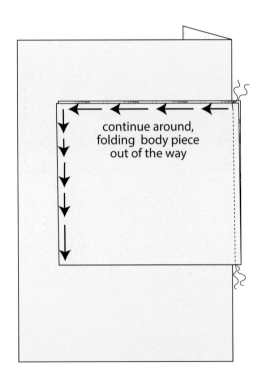

continue around, folding body piece out of the way

Figure 25

Lining Small Pocket

37 Fold RECTANGLE H in half, right sides facing. Sew the perimeter with a ¼" (6mm) seam allowance, leaving a 4" (10cm) opening for turning. (Fig. 26) Turn right-side out. Press flat. Fold the Pocket divisions and press to create a crease to use as a sewing guide. Topstitch the top edge at ¼" (6mm). Fold in the seam allowance of the opening and pin the opening closed. (Fig. 27)

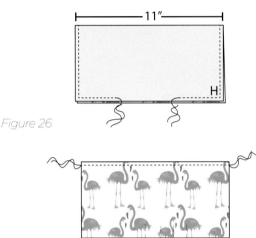

Figure 26

Figure 27

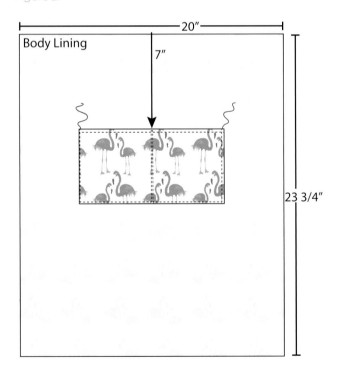

Body Lining

Figure 28

38 Center the Pocket 7" (18cm) down from the top edge of the right side of the remaining Body Lining piece. From the right side, topstitch the two sides, bottom and on each side of the creased line at ⅛" (3mm). This will close the opening at the bottom and create pocket divisions. (Fig. 28)

Zipper Strip

39 Align one long side of RECTANGLE J with the top of one Body Lining piece, right sides facing. Position the long zipper between the two pieces with the front side of the zipper facing Rectangle J. The teeth from the top of the zipper should begin 1" (2.5cm) from the edges of Rectangle J. Sew with a ¼" (6mm) seam allowance. (Fig. 29) Turn right-side out with wrong sides facing and the zipper extended beyond the fabric pieces. Topstitch at ⅛" (3mm) and again at ⅜" (1cm). (Fig. 30)

40 Repeat for the other side of the zipper using the remaining Rectangle J and Lining Piece. (Fig. 31) Cut off the overhanging portion of zipper flush with the body pieces. Whipstitch by machine ½" (1.3cm) from the cut to reinforce the zipper.

Figure 30

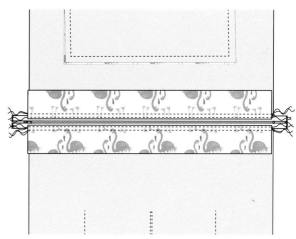

Figure 31

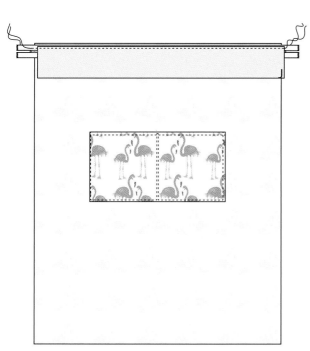

Figure 29

41 Align the lower 20" (51cm) ends of the Body Lining pieces, right sides facing, and sew with a ½" (1.3cm) seam allowance. The side with the zipper pocket is the back of the bag.

42 Align the Body Exterior piece with one side of the Zipper Strip, right sides facing. Sew with a ½" (1.3cm) seam allowance. (Fig. 32) Turn right-side out. With the seam allowance folded toward the Zipper Strip, topstitch through all layers at ⅛" (3mm) and again at ⅜" (1cm) on the Zipper Strip side.

Tip: Some of these steps are a little easier if you unzip the zipper.

43 Repeat for the back of the bag.

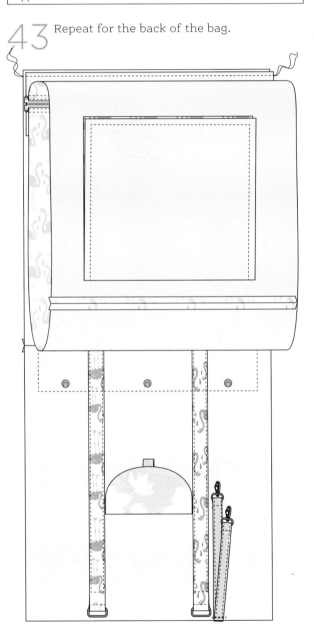

Figure 32

Assembling the Body

44 Pin the Body Exterior and Lining layers together along the sides.

> Tip: It is necessary to ease a little because the Lining side is slightly smaller than the Exterior side. Make tiny clips in the seam allowance of the Lining if needed to help with the easing. The Lining is smaller than the Exterior to reduce the interior bulk.

45 Turn the lining side out. Align the Body to the Side, exterior sides facing. Begin by aligning the center bottom and tops to the respective pieces. Make ⅜" (1cm) clips every ½" (1.3cm) along the raw edge of the Body in areas that will be aligned with curves of the Side. Use the clips in the fabric to allow for neat curves. Sew with a ½" (1.3cm) seam allowance. (Fig. 33) Trim the seam allowance to ¼" (6mm). Trim the Soft and Stable in the seam allowance to ⅛" (3mm).

46 Repeat for the other Side.

Binding (Seam Finish)

47 Open the bias tape. Fold the end of the bias tape ½" (1.3cm), wrong sides facing, and press. This will be the clean start of the seam finish. Begin at the bottom of the bag. Align the first manufactured fold of the bias tape with the Body seam on the Lining side. Pin the perimeter. Use the stretch of the bias to ease evenly. Overlap the bias tape ½" (1.3cm) at the end. Sew along this fold.

48 Fold the bias tape around the seam allowance so it overlaps the previous stitching by about ⅛" (3mm) and stitch in the ditch. (Fig. 34)

49 Repeat for the other Side. Turn right-side out.

Figure 33

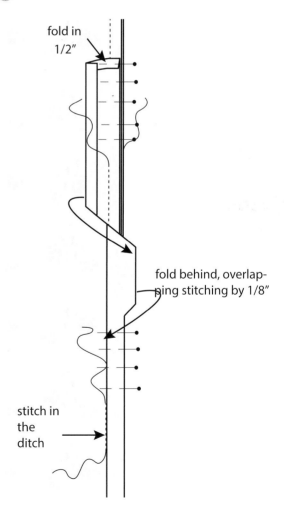

fold in 1/2"

fold behind, overlapping stitching by 1/8"

stitch in the ditch

Figure 34

Handles and Shoulder Strap

50 Fuse the fusible fleece to the wrong side of the SHOULDER STRAP and both HANDLES as illustrated. Fold the wrong sides facing and press as illustrated. (Fig. 35) The finished width should be 1¼" (3.2cm). Topstitch both sides at ⅛" (3mm), hiding all raw edges.

51 Thread each end through a metal rectangle for the Handles, or swivel hook for the Shoulder Strap, overlapping 1¼" (3.2cm). Topstitch at ⅛" (3mm). (Fig. 36) One Handle is for the front and one for the back of the bag. Snap a swivel hook onto a D-ring on each side of the bag and a couple of charms on the Charm Hanger.

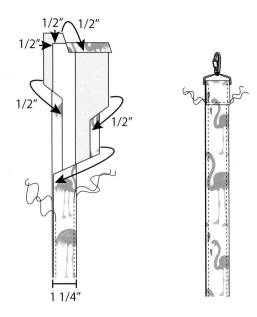

Figure 35   *Figure 36*

Resources

The tools and materials used in this book can be found at your local fabric store or favorite online retailer. For more information on specific items used, contact the manufacturers listed here.

Beacon Adhesives
www.beacon1.com
527 Glue

By Annie
www.byannie.com
Soft and Stable; sew-in magnets

Coats & Clark
www.makeitcoats.com
zippers

Dritz
www.dritz.com
covered buttons; cording; grommets

E-6000
eclecticproducts.com
glue

Pellon
www.pellonprojects.com
stabilizers

Riley Blake Designs
www.rileyblakedesigns.com
fabric

Wrights
www.simplicity.com
bias tape

Hardware Kits

The following hardware kits are available at www.golightlysewingstudio.com. Note that installation tools are not included in kits.

Boutique Day Purse
Purse Hardware:
4 O-rings, 1¼"
2 sets of sew-in magnets

Changeable Cover Hardware:
4 purse feet, 14mm
2 sets of sew-in magnets
1 center post buckle, 1" (2.5cm)
1 eyelet set, ¼" (6mm)

Day-by-Day Wallet
2 sets of invisible sew-in magnets

Double-Take Clutch
1 center post buckle, ¾" (2cm)
2 rectangles, ¾" (2cm)
3 eyelet sets, ¼" (6mm)

Farmer's Market Tote
1 set of exterior magnets
4 center post buckles, 1" (2.5cm)
4 eyelet sets, ¼" (6mm)

Free-Spirit Drawstring Purse
8 eyelet sets, $\frac{7}{16}$" (1.1cm)
5 eyelet sets, ¼" (6mm)
1 center post buckle, 1" (2.5cm)
2 rectangles, 1" (2.5cm)

On-the-Go Bag
1 swivel hook, 1¼" (3.2cm)
2 rectangles, 1¼" (3.2cm)
2 slides, 1¼" (3.2cm)
4 purse feet, 18mm
1 swivel hook, ½" (1.3cm)
Drawstring closure option: 1 metal D-ring, 1¼"
   (3.2cm)

Lunch Date Clutch
2 sets of exterior magnets
2 purse frames, 3½" × 10" (9cm × 25.5cm)
2 swivel hooks, ¾" (2cm)
2 D-rings, ¾" (1.3cm)

Park Bench Ruffle Purse
4 O-rings, 1¼" (3.2cm)
1 set of exterior magnets

Piccadilly Purse
6 O-rings, 1¼" (3.2cm)
2 swivel hooks, 1" (2.5cm)
4 purse feet, 18mm
2 swivel hooks, ½" (1.3cm)

Province Travel Bag
2 sets of exterior magnets
2 D-rings, 1¼" (3.2cm)
4 rectangles, 1¼" (3.2cm)
2 swivel hooks, 1¼" (3.2cm)
6 purse feet, 18mm
2 swivel hooks, ½" (1.3cm)

Serendipity Purse
1 twist lock unit, 2⅛" × 1⅜" (55mm × 35mm)
26 beads, 25mm
28 closed jump rings, 10mm

Index

a content + ecommerce company

www.fwcommunity.com

20 19 18 17 16   5 4 3 2 1

Distributed in Canada by Fraser Direct
100 Armstrong Avenue
Georgetown, ON, Canada L7G 5S4
Tel: (905) 877-4411

Distributed in the U.K. and Europe by
F&W MEDIA INTERNATIONAL
Brunel House, Newton Abbot, Devon, TQ12 4PU, England
Tel: (+44) 1626 323200, Fax: (+44) 1626 323319
E-mail: enquiries@fwmedia.com

Distributed in Australia by Capricorn Link
P.O. Box 704, S. Windsor NSW, 2756 Australia
Tel: (02) 4560 1600, Fax: (02) 4577 5288
E-mail: books@capricornlink.com.au

SRN: T6749
ISBN-13: 978-1-4402-4420-9

Edited by Christine Doyle
Project managed by Noel Rivera
Designed by Corrie Schaffeld
Production coordinated by Bryan Davidson
Illustrations by Mary Gavilanes

Photoshoot produced by MBN Productions
Hair by Kia McMillan
Makeup by Makeup By Naz
Jewelry styling by Beth Baumer
Wardrobe styling by Naz Madaen
Photography by Harper Point Photography, Nathan Rega
Models: Ellen Hancock and Jessica Peterson

We make every effort to ensure the accuracy of our instructions, but errors occasionally occur. Errata can be found at www.sewingdaily.com/errata.

About the Illustrator

Mary Ashley Gavilanes is a mother to three young children by day, and an illustrator and pattern designer by night. As an editor, illustrator and pattern designer for *Golightly Sewing Studio* since 2011, she has collaborated on many patterns for clothing, bags and accessories.

Since childhood, sewing has been a creative outlet for Mary, who especially enjoys designing and piecing beautiful, complex quilts. While obtaining her B.S. in Biotechnology Business at Brigham Young University, creating intricately detailed diagrams became part of her learning method to piece together difficult concepts. The challenge of learning pattern illustration and design brought these two passions together.

mary@golightlysewingstudio.com

Dedication

I dedicate this book to the light of my life, my grandbabies: Sean, Caleb, Skyleigh, Kylee, Royal, Eli, Johnny, Thomas, River, Lilia, Avery, Cassidy and all the treasures still to come.

About the Author

Michelle Golightly knew she had ideas and a method the industry appreciated when her first bag pattern was invited to be in *Patchwork Spezial* magazine. Her patterns and designs have also been featured in the popular *100 Layer Cake* blog and the Bernina Virtual Clubs, and she has been a featured pattern designer with Riley Blake Designs.

Michelle received a B.F.A. in piano performance and pedagogy from Brigham Young University. From concerts in the park to world-renowned recital halls and parades down cobblestone streets in tiny villages, she performed as a fiddler, violinist and pianist throughout Asia, Canada, the United States and Europe. The artistic works she has seen during her international travels continue to inspire her to be an artist in her own corner of the world, help others to be motivated to create extraordinary things and spread the message, "You can do *anything* you put your mind to."

michelle@golightlysewingstudio.com

Acknowledgments

Thank you to the many people who have helped me along the way! Friend and mentor, Lila Tueller, who shared her experience and resources without limit. Chelsea Andersen for her cheerful encouragement and support. Amanda Herring for sharing the fruits of her fabulous artistry. Cindi Cloward and Jina Barney from Riley Blake Designs for generously providing fabric for this book. Amelia Johanson and Fons&Porter for seeking us out for this project.

My bags, in all of their refining stages, have been run through our "focus groups"—actually, any woman walking in or near my home or workplace is badgered for an opinion. This group includes my piano students, their moms, university students and faculty, supporting neighborhood family, pattern testers—Megan, Mary, Rachel, Ann, Karen, Cheryl, Breta, Jeni, Brittney, Roma and Kellie—and the women in my family who thoughtfully responded to my constant interrogation about every detail of every creation. I am grateful to Megan and Josh for their graphic design counsel and artistic photography. The men in our family deserve recognition for their patience, support, and "picking-up-the-slack" skills. Thanks to my husband, Kyle, who believes in me.

A special thanks to my collaborator and daughter, Mary Gavilanes. She is not only my partner in ideas, but she meticulously creates these beautiful and helpful illustrations with accuracy, clarity, perspective and artistry. Mary is the interpreter and filter to my wordiness; in her opinion, if something can be described with 5 words and one illustration, why use 50 words? My readers should be thanking her as well. We regularly share 3 a.m. texts and conversations because those are the magic, uninterrupted hours of creativity...except when her newborn baby girl doesn't abide by these rules.

Thank you, Dad, Leland Briggs, who believed I could do anything. Thank you, Mom, Mary Briggs, for teaching me to sew.

Try these other fantastic bag titles!

The Bag Making Bible
by Lisa Lam
978-0-71533-624-3
$24.99

The Bag Making Bible offers a technique-led approach to sewing your own designer bags and purses. Each chapter is fully illustrated with helpful color photography and ends with a unique, step-by-step project that builds the ultimate handbag wardrobe. Full-size pull-out patterns require no copying and let you get started right away! Each lovely bag design is fun to make and will be loved for years to come.

Sew Serendipity Bags
by Kay Whitt
978-1-44021-415-8
$29.99

With full instructions for twelve bags—and with a few clever variations thrown in—there are plenty of options to choose from in this delightful book from designer Kay Whitt! Pick a handbag that is sweet, sleek or funky, or check out some of the other great designs: a flirty little backpack, the perfect lunch bag, convenient shopping bags and handy task-oriented bags (whether that task involves a laptop, gym clothes or diapers). Each design is easy to adapt to your style.